REFLECTIONS

Best Wishes & Thanks Hope you enjoy book

Bert Verey

REFLECTIONS
A TRILOGY OF MEMORIES

The life story of Bert Verney

HALSGROVE

First published in 1996 by Halsgrove

Copyright © 1996 A.W. Verney

All rights reserved. No part of this publication may be reproduced in any form or by any means without the prior permission of the copyright holder.

British Library Cataloguing in Print Data

CIP Data for this book is available from the British Library

ISBN 1 874448 20 5

HALSGROVE
Publishing, Media and Distribution

Halgrove House
Lower Moor Way
Tiverton
Devon EX16 6ss
Tel: 01884 243242
Fax: 01884 243242

The cover illustrations are: front cover main picture - the author hard at work on this book, in the garden at Verdala with his wife, May. Inset picture is of Scraggy the Spaniel. The back cover picture shows John, the author's son with a prize catch, a 25lb salmon; Scraggy looking on.

Printed in Great Britain by the Devonshire Press, Torquay

CONTENTS

ACKNOWLEDGEMENTS 4
FOREWORD 5

PART ONE

CHAPTER ONE 7
CHAPTER TWO 12
CHAPTER THREE 19
CHAPTER FOUR 29
CHAPTER FIVE 44
CHAPTER SIX 54
CHAPTER SEVEN 56
CHAPTER EIGHT 58
CHAPTER NINE 61
CHAPTER TEN 64
CHAPTER ELEVEN 67
CHAPTER TWELVE 81
CHAPTER THIRTEEN 82
CHAPTER FOURTEEN 84
CHAPTER FIFTEEN 85
CHAPTER SIXTEEN 89
CHAPTER SEVENTEEN 93
CHAPTER EIGHTEEN 102

PART TWO
THE STORY OF SCRAGGY - A GREAT DOG 107

PART THREE
POEMS- REFLECTIONS OF A LIFE 123

ACKNOWLEDGEMENTS

The Author wishes to thank all those who have helped with the production of this book: My wife, for her patience and many hours of solitude. Thanks also to R. L. Knight, S. H. Bath, *News of the World*, *Sporting Life*, Beaford Archives and many personal friends for help with the photographs; Jill Stanbury for doing the drawings; Simon Grimshaw for the plans, and finally to Diana Thomas for the typing and collating of material. Special thanks to all those who contributed to the costs of publication.

The author has written this book with sensitivity. He is a romantic but with his feet firmly set on the ground, and very much a family man with hopes and dreams. If you believe in destiny, then there was an obvious path laid out for him, which he had to follow.

Proceeds from the sale of this book will be donated to the North Devon Hospice.

FOREWORD

Today is my birthday. September 5th, 1995. I am seventy-four years of age. It is also another great milestone, as today my wife, May, and I have been married for fifty years. It is our Golden Wedding anniversary. We both felt overcome and very emotional. The flowers and cards and good wishes and kind messages were overwhelming.

Today it's time to pause and reflect of days and years gone by. I feel I am sitting on a seat, half-way up a hill. Below is a beautiful valley stretching away to a distant past. A long, silver line threads through the valley - the route of my life, the memories, the clouds, the sunshine, the sorrow and joy come flooding back. Looking over my shoulder up the hill, covered in low cloud, giving no clue of what lies ahead. One thing is certain, somewhere in the cloud life's last greatest adventure is still to come.

I can't forecast the future - I don't know what it will be - so I will tell you some of the things I remember of the past.

A.W. VERNEY
NORTH DEVON

A single-masted barque tied up at Barnstaple Quay in the early 1900s. The author and his brother saw ships like this while on their trips into the town.

The interior of the Pannier Market.

CHAPTER ONE
TRANSPORT

The first means of transport I can remember was around 1927-28, the horse and trap. The horse, Tommy, was about fifteen hands, a chestnut gelding and a real beauty. The trap was a two-wheeled carriage, the seat the full width of the trap (5ft. 4ins. wide and about 2ft. 6ins. from the front edge). A space of about 6ft. was at the back for luggage, market hamper or casual seating. Long metal springs acted as shock-absorbers, with wheels of wood sometimes clad with hard solid rubber, but mostly by an iron band.

We had a leopardskin rug, waterproof and warm, to cover our legs and thighs in wet, and cold weather. Also a huge, black umbrella under which we crouched on wet journeys. Often used for visiting our grandparents who lived at Braunton, some eight miles distant.

The journey took about one and a quarter hours, or perhaps a little less. Grandad, although retired, had ten acres of land, a nice house some twenty years old up a gravel drive, consisting of small white or off-white pebbles. He still kept a cow for his milk, butter and cream and a couple of pigs to eat the household waste. They drank the surplus skimmed milk.

When visiting on a summer day, my brother and I would slip away to Vellator, some half a mile away, to see the sailing boats with one or two masts, tied up there.

Various cargo was unloaded there. Manure, timber, coal and many other items. There were many mallard in the dykes, and sometimes swans. In the small stream, the Caen, it had a kind of fish ladder which was always teeming with brown trout. Not very big - two to six inches, but a lovely sight. There was always something of interest at Vellator — but I am wandering away from my subject, means of transport.

It was surprising how snug and warm one was, even in the foulest of weather. Beneath the rug and the brolly, snuggled between our parents, often fast asleep by the time we arrived home. I don't know how the horse or driver could see the way on dark nights, when the lights were one lamp on each side of the trap, lit by a large candle. As the candle burnt, it was pushed up by a spring. I think the only reason for the light, was to warn other people of your approach and not, to see where you were going.

On market days the horse and trap were used to take my parents to Barnstaple, some three miles distant. My Mother used to have a stall (as most farmer's wives did) in the Pannier Market. A beautiful and artistic building some 100 yards long, with posts holding up the roof every eleven feet, or so. The roof, itself solid, fifteen feet each side as far out as the posts, then it went up some ten feet and was made up of glass panes fitted into wooden

The pony and jingo.

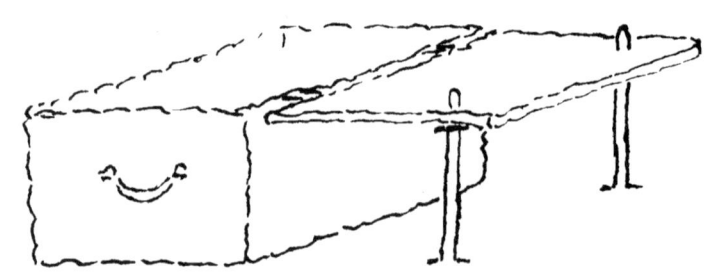

Market wicket hamper, showing how the lid was used as a table.

frames. The stalls would consist of a large hamper, made of wicker, interwoven, some three feet deep, four feet wide and five feet long, with handles for carrying at each end. There were always men waiting to help carry, when you arrived at the market, and others who took charge of the horse and trap, stabling the horse and housing the trap in one of the many inns in the town.

To display one's goods, the hamper was opened on a hinged top. The far end of the top had two small holes, through which two stays were placed. These took the weight of the lid on their cross-pieces. The lid then became a table, for displaying one's goods, i.e. butter, cream, often a boiling hen, rabbit, sprouts, peas, beans, apples and at pig killing time (hog's pudding and pork sausages). A set of scales was always carried to weigh goods.

The market, with all its stalls, was a great sight to see and to the many visitors to North Devon, a must. It became terribly crowded during the summer months. In the winter it was bitterly cold. Sliding doors, down one side, would be opened, letting in the chill winds and allowing entrance to all the stalls. The main business of the market was done by one o'clock, when one would throw a rug over the stall and do one's own shopping in the town, and perhaps have a meal in one of the many cafes. Nothing was ever stolen from the stalls, although left unattended for long periods. At the far end of the Pannier Market was the Corn Exchange, where farmers and merchants carried out their business.

Outside the market was Butchers Row, with some thirty butchers' shops displaying huge carcasses of beef, lamb and pigs. These too were a magnificent sight, with their displays of meat. At Christmas poultry, holly and mistletoe were displayed. But there - I have been wandering away from transport once again.

We had a governess to teach us at that time (because of my sister, who was unable to go to school because of her infirmity). This teacher, a parson's wife, used to come in a pony and jingo (in other places called a 'jingle'). This was a small light trap with cockpit, some five feet by five feet, with seats all around.

Butchers' Row outside the Barnstaple Pannier Market, taken in the 1920s. It was here that, as a boy, the author saw the magnificent Christmas displays of meat and game arranged outside each shop.

Then there was the hackney carriage, which could be hired from stables in Barnstaple, for special occasions such as weddings, funerals, etc. These were four-wheeled carriages, where the driver sat outside, whilst the cabin, slung between front and back wheels, would hold four to six people.

Then, of course, there was just the horse, which many people rode with the aid of a saddle, and many ladies with side-saddles (with one ordinary stirrup). The top side of the saddle had a 'V' shape jutting out where the right leg was supported above the knee. I think this was done because ladies wore skirts, in those days, and could not sit astride a horse. It must have been rather uncomfortable riding in that manner.

Many farm-yards had walls of stone with large stones sticking out (to some five feet in height). These 'upping stocks' were there to enable these ladies to mount the horse and also to assist some elderly men!

This may have given you some idea of some of the ways of transport, by horse.

Then came the car. I remember our first car, bought in 1929: an Austin 12 h.p. tourer, with convertible hood and celluloid windows; a large hooter outside, large spoked wheels and a windscreen made of glass. I cannot remember if it had windscreen wipers. It was, I believe, started by cranking it with a handle, and I think the lights were run by some sort of battery or dynamo. I know how proud we were when riding in that car. We felt like royalty!

I remember going on Sunday School outings at about that time, in cumbersome buses. Very solid

Off for the day - a charabanc outing in North Devon c. 1920.

and with solid, hard rubber tyres. Top speed was about fifteen miles per hour, and it provided a very bumpy and uncomfortable ride. Still, it did its job. and we arrived there safely at our destination of Ilfracombe or Woolacombe, some sixteen miles distant.

The fastest and easiest way to travel was by steam train. Every village adjoining the railway had its own station. The journey from Exeter to Barnstaple took well over an hour, nearly two, because of the many stops on the journey of just under forty miles. Many goods were carted by train:. animal foodstuffs, manure, building materials, clay from the clay pits, and coal were but a few of the commodities using the railways.

We kept a large waggon, pulled by a pair of horses, whose only use was carting foods from the railway station to the farm. This included corn, cattle-cake, manure and, sometimes, timber.

These were the main means of transport in the Twenties and early Thirties. Rather slow, but pretty reliable.

Barnstaple Square c. 1910 showing the carriages for hire. The bicycle was also a popular form of transport, despite the steep hills in North Devon.

A 'Growler' stands outside the Malt Scoop Inn, Merton, North Devon. This type of carriage was the Rolls Royce of its day.

CHAPTER TWO
MY FAMILY

Our family comprised Mum, Dad, sister, older brother and myself. Mum was an only child and her parents were very strict and very religious. Grandfather was choirmaster at the local chapel. Very musical. He was an excellent farmer and everything had to be just so. Neat and tidy and clean. He had the best herd of pedigree Devons (Ruby Reds) of his day. He won numerous prizes at all the leading shows and many of the trophies we still have today: cups, rose bowls, tea services, lamps and coffee sets. He also won many other trophies for sheep, corn and root crops. He was a great man in the farming world, well thought of and respected. Mum, being the only child, inherited the farm and his large collection of trophies at his death, at the early age of sixty-three. He died of a brain tumor. I never really knew Mum's parents, as they were both dead by the time I was two years old. I remember my Father's parents, kindly, caring and enjoying their retirement at Braunton. Though, during the latter years, Granny was bed-ridden but was lucky enough to be looked after by her unmarried daughter.

My Father was a very good farmer - mixed farming: beef, sheep and a little arable. He was always on the look-out for a bargain, and bought odd pieces of land and a couple of farms. I suppose, leaving out 'Overton', which belonged to Mother, he owned about 470 acres of land by 1945. Much of this he let to young people, giving them a chance to start farming on their own. Father was hard but very fair, always ready to listen to the other side of the story. His word was his bond and he looked after his workers and always paid a few shillings above basic wage. (Twenty-nine shillings or thirty shillings for a hard week's work - Father paid thirty-three shillings per week). He was happy in the thought that he gave others a chance to start farming.

Mother was a very busy person, running the house, even though she had a maid and old Annie to help. She had to plan meals for eight people, their washing and preparing vegtables for market. Making butter and cream and hog's pudding, etc. But a large amount of her time was spent in looking after my sister, a polio victim, who had lost the use of both legs and had to be carried everywhere, and waited upon. Mother felt it was her duty, and rarely trusted other people with this task. She had to share the time she had left, between her husband and my brother and me. She loved us all very dearly, her task must have been nigh impossible.

My sister, as I have told you, was a victim of polio at four and a half years old. Despite this crippling handicap, I have never heard her moan or complain, although she must have felt terribly

A proud Mum and Dad with the family.

left out on many occasions. She bore her handicap with great courage and dignity. She learned to paint in oils, to play the piano and to sing, and became a very good cook. She made the best of the limited life she had.

My older brother was a rather reserved and quiet sort of chap. He was brilliant at school, and matriculated with ease. He enjoyed his sport, i.e. cricket, rugby and football, although not brilliant at any. When he left school, he became Father's

My sister, brother and I.

right-hand on the farm and I am sure would have made a very good farmer, indeed.

We did many things together. I suppose he was a sort of an idol to me. I have many happy memories of games we played - of our days rabbiting, of the good times we had at the Young Farmers Club and of the pranks we played on other people (always good fun, nothing really nasty), of the interest we both had in politics. Perhaps it was partly the girls we met and the fun we had, more than serious politics. I am sure the leading figures of our local Conservative Party thought of him as a future candidate and perhaps their M.P.

As for myself, I never did very well at school though I did quite well at sport, i.e. rugby, cricket and athletics, although I could never really sprint and was more than useful over distances of half a mile and over. Very good at steeple-chasing. I was lucky to have a good singing voice, and was often asked to sing solos at school, and chapel choir. I also had a flair for acting, and was often asked to read poetry to class at school, because of my ability to get the best and true meanings out of lines. I had two great write-ups by drama critics in the local paper, for a couple of roles I played in local productions.

If the war had not come, perhaps I would have tried the acting and musical world for a career. Perhaps I would have succeeded, perhaps not, but I would have tried. Sadly I shall never know.

There was one thing that I enjoyed and did without my brother, and that was fishing. Although all I caught in those days were mullet, dabs and eels, it was still great fun. They were hard but happy days in the late twenties and early thirties.

Those were my immediate family, but I think I should include Annie Oliver. She had been with the family for a great number of years, having had a daughter out of wedlock, which was a great disgrace and sin in those days. She was glad to have a home, a job and refuge. She was a really lovely old lady, though she suffered terribly from asthma. She made the best of her disability, always trying to earn her keep in small ways. She could no longer do the heavy or hard work but was a great help to Mum, peeling potatoes and apples and washing dishes. She always lit the hearth fire and fried the breakfast for eight people: fat bacon from our own pigs, eggs, and potatoes left over from the day before, and often batter pancakes. If anyone wanted toast, it had to be toasted on long-handled forks (about two feet, six inches) over the open fire. The taste was superb, and when covered with home-made butter, jam or marmalade, was really a meal on its own. She cooked or fried the breakfast in a huge frying pan, holding ten eggs at a time, balanced on a brandis over an open fire. So we all started the day with a fine, large and tasty breakfast.

Farm workers worked long hours, from 7am to 5.30pm with a twenty-minute break for lunch (10am to 10.20am). An hour for midday meal (1pm to 2 pm) five days a week. On Saturdays it was 7am to 1 pm and on Sundays two to three hours (feeding stock and bedding-up in the winter - in the summer, half an hour, seeing that all stock were in good health). No holidays, just Christmas Day, Boxing Day and Good Friday, which was usually spent planting the large gardens, which supplied them with vegetables for the year. Most workers had a cottage, rent free. They kept a few hens in a house and pen in the corner of the garden. (House usually was made of flattened, empty tar barrels or old and galvanized rusty sheets. Many also kept a pig, as most farm cottages had a sty where one could be kept. They were allowed to plant one cwt bag of seed potatoes in the farmer's field; usually allowed one pint of milk daily, given apples at picking time and allowed to catch a rabbit, when they needed one, and allowed swede or turnips from the field. The wages, in the late twenties and thirties, as said previously, were from twenty-eight to thirty shillings per week. Many farmers paid a couple of bob more.

Beer was then about two old pence a pint. Cigarettes were six old pence for ten, Woodbines were five for two old pence and pipe tobacco, four old pence an ounce. One could get a good-sized hunk of meat for two shillings and six old pence; eggs varied from six old pence to one shilling a dozen. Herrings, caught off Clovelly, could be bought in Barnstaple at twelve for six old pence. So, although wages were very low, food was very cheap, thus enabling these people to somehow exist with no money for luxuries. Yet, even under these conditions, they seemed happy and content with life. What a change today (for the better). Yes, very much so, and yet the people are more discontent than they were in those hard times!

The boy living-in at the time, was called Willy Hewitt. A very nice, honest and hard-working lad. He was clever with his hands and could do most jobs on the farm, with great skill and speed.

I include Annie and Willy as part of the family because we would all sit around the great kitchen table, as one large family. They joined in the conversations and laughter. Although they were paid workers, there was really no 'them and us'. We ate the same food and did the same work. So the best word to describe how we lived and carried on, was 'we'.

Kitchen utensils and hearth furniture found in most farm and cottages when the author was a boy.

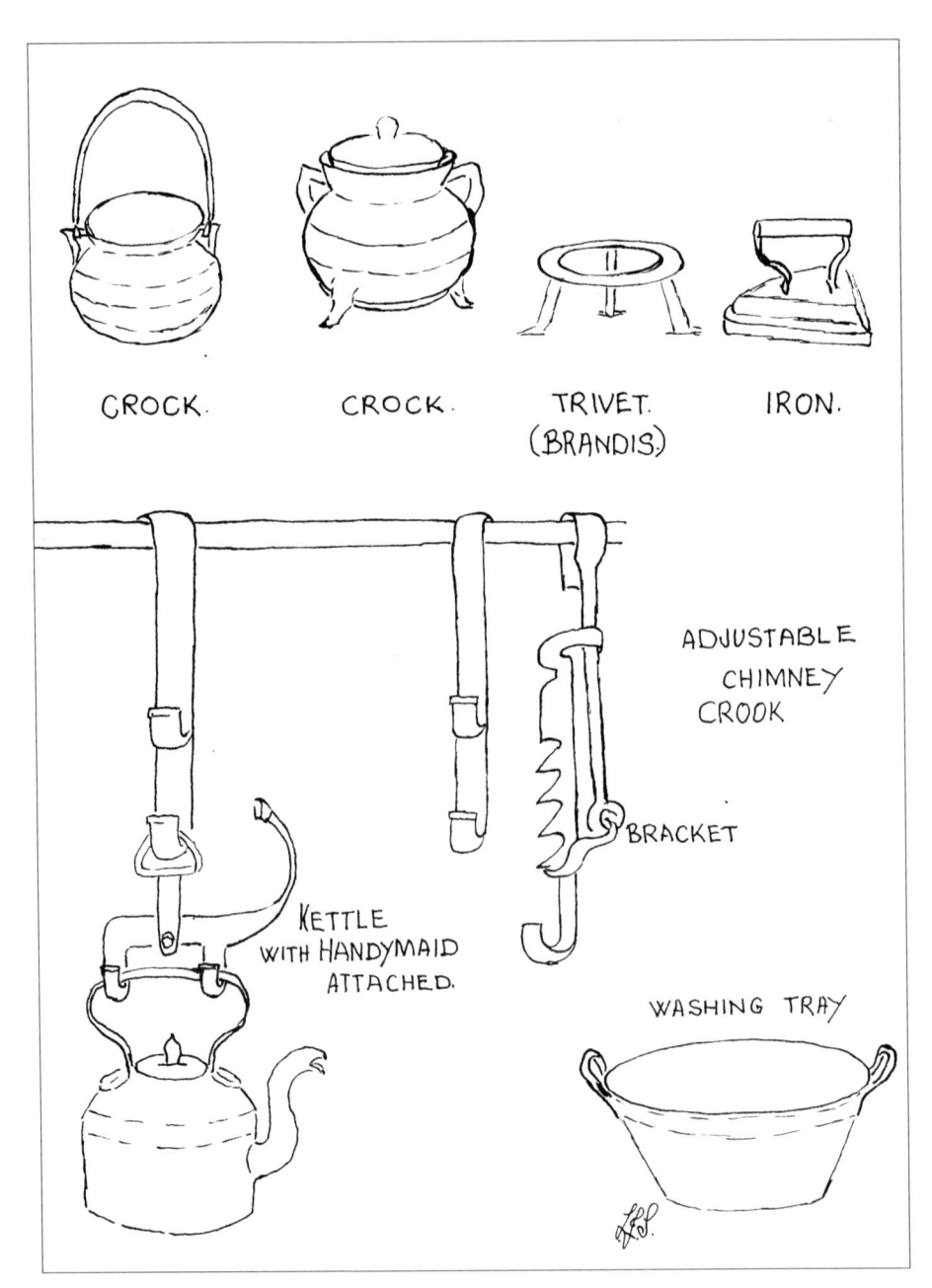

CROCK.

CROCK.

TRIVET. (BRANDIS).

IRON.

ADJUSTABLE CHIMNEY CROOK

BRACKET

KETTLE WITH HANDYMAID ATTACHED.

WASHING TRAY

The eighth member of the household was a girl called Bessie, a hard-working quiet girl, always willing to learn the ways of a farmer's wife which stood her well in years to come, as she became a farmer's wife herself. She is now in her eighties and loves to talk of her days at Overton.

When we had visitors, though, they stayed in the kitchen. The visitors and the five of us would either go to the morning room or the drawing room. That was the only time we parted, except on some evenings when they had some of their friends in for a chat and game of darts, cards or dominoes. Then they would remain in the kitchen. They would never join us in the evenings unless asked to do so, which they usually were.

Annie was a second Mum to me. Mother was glad to let her take me off her hands, knowing I was safe in her care, thus giving her a little time of her own and a chance to take a well-earned rest.

A TIME TO REFLECT: A DAY OUT WITH ANNIE

One day, I will never forget; Annie (well into her seventies) took me to Ilfracombe on a steam train. I don't remember how we got to the station but I think Dad must have taken us there, by car. I was so excited I was going to ride on a train.

This was the first time, and it was a great thrill to hear the chuff of its engine as it started its journey. To see the smoke and steam drifting back past the window and to smell the smoke and to hear the rattle and clatter of the wheels, as they sped along the track. Then to hear the power of the engine as it put on full power to climb the steep gradient, at Morthoe. It was a great experience - one I shall never forget.

My second mother - Annie and friend

From the Station, on top of a hill, we walked to Ilfracombe some quarter of a mile below. Annie, in her best black boots, long black skirt and black blouse with black straw hat to match. I do not remember what I was wearing. Probably an open necked shirt and short-sleeved pullover, baggy pair of trousers, ankle-length socks and shoes. I remember wearing clothes like that about that time. We must have looked some sight!

I remember she bought me a lovely boat, it was a copy of a (then modern) liner. It cost five shillings; a lot of money in those days. Having bought the boat, we had to find somewhere to try it out, so we made for the Tunnel Beach. The only way to get there was through a tunnel, in the rocks (hence its name). We spent the rest of the morning there sailing the boat in the rock-pools, of which there were many.

Having tried out the boat, Annie decided it was time to have someting to eat. We made our way back to town along the front, and chose a cafe opposite the Capstone, the large hill right on the sea front. Annie ordered chicken and salad, which turned out to be a very bad choice. The chicken had gone off (turned bad) so we could not eat it. She did not complain, and I was not old enough to do so. What cheats they were, to serve bad food to a very old and frail lady and a skinny little boy. She bought me an ice-cream, paid the bill, and left. It was now getting time to catch the train home.

It must have taken poor old Annie, with her breathing problems, at least half an hour to cover the half a mile up the hill to the station. She had to have many stops on the way. At last we reached the station, with plenty of time to spare.

What a day of mixed fortunes. The exciting train ride, the terrible food we could not eat. But Annie had taken her boy to the seaside. They had both ridden in the train and he had a lovely boat, which he would treasure for years to come. If that's what she thought, how right she was!

GEORGE AND THE CAT!

A lady living in one of our cottages had a mania for cats. I think she had about twelve to sixteen, at this particular time.

George used to go shopping in Barnstaple. His only means of transport was the bus, as it was for the owner of the cats. This lady, knowing that it was George's day for the shopping and being unwell herself, asked George if he could drop off a cat at the vets. She said he would be expecting it. He could leave the basket with the vet and she would pick it up sometime later, when she was feeling better, and in town.

So off George went to catch the bus, about half a mile away. He could not see much sense in taking the cat to the vet when he could do the job painlessly and quickly, and thus save the owner the vet's fee, because she was not too well blessed with cash. So he opened the basket, held the cat in one hand and with a clean and swift blow with his walking stick, all was over. He would put the basket in a field, pick it up on the way home and bury the cat in his garden. That would be his good turn for the day.

When he got home, he duly buried the cat in his garden. The next morning he told the cat owner what he had done. He had done it very humanely - the cat had felt nothing and he had saved her the vet's fee. This news brought tears to the lady's eyes. George, seeing this, made a hasty retreat. What he did not know, and what she never told him, was that the vet was not going to put the cat down, but was going to neuter him! As George was so pleased with what he had done and thinking he had done her a good turn, she had not got the heart to tell him the truth. And he never knew!

CHAPTER THREE
THE HOUSE - OUR HOME AND ITS WORKINGS

Overton was a strange-shaped house, having been built-on at least three different times. The oldest part, an old longhouse, was built with cob. The roof was of thatch and the timbers in the roof, still there (half oak trees with the bark still on one side), hard as iron and held together with wooden oak pins. This wood is still in perfect condition, despite being many hundreds of years old.

Baron de Overton lived there in the twelfth century. The old longhouse could have been there at that time, but was probably built a couple of hundred years later. The roof is now of slate. The wings were built on, i.e. large hall and sitting room on the south side; large kitchen, salting soom and dairy on the north side, giving the house the shape of a cross).

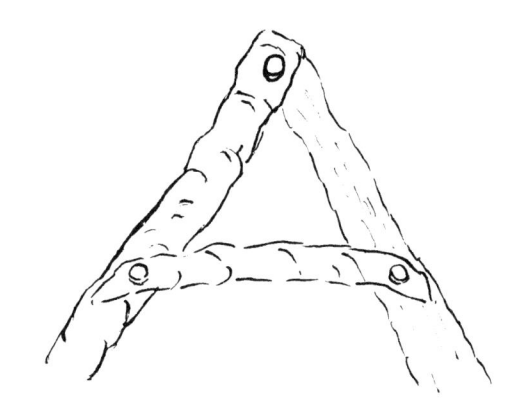

HALF OAK TREE ROOF TRUSS.

Overton - our family home.

The house had six double-bedrooms; one bedroom had a four-poster bed. A bathroom and separate toilet upstairs and downstairs, the sitting room, dining room, hall, front kitchen, office, salting room, dairy and large kitchen. The smallest of these rooms was about fourteen feet by sixteen feet. The largest, some eighteen feet by twenty feet. There were grates (fire-places) in five of the bedrooms and all the downstairs rooms. There were two staircases to the upper floor and many passages to join the rooms. An upstairs loo and downstairs loo with hand basins.

LAMPS AND LIGHTING

Lighting (such as it was) was a real problem, very poor compared with today. It meant much hard work in preparing the lamps, keeping the globes clean, trimming the wicks and filling with oil. If you were lucky, you could see to read within a radius of six to eight feet. The flame, at the top of the wick, would be about one inch to one-and-a-half inches, so you can imagine what light was obtained from a flame of this size. The wicks had to be trimmed daily and usually the globes needed polishing, to help give the best light possible. Oil was the only means of fuelling the lamps (no electricity or gas) in the country districts. To go to bed or to the bathroom, one had one's own candlestick and candle. The light given by a single candle was all you had to shave with, and if you wanted to read in bed, you had to hold the book within a couple of feet of the candle, to be able to see! These two methods of lighting were messy, and the grease had to be cleaned off daily.

A little later, came the Aladdin with a mantle which, when lit, provided a much better light. Then came the Tilley. When you pumped it, a fine spray of fuel (again oil) went on to the mantle. The more pressure you put into the base with the pump, the brighter the light. In fact, the light was quite good. The mantle had to be warmed, with a clip containing pads soaked in methylated spirit. When lit, these were clipped on the stem of the lamp, just below the mantle.

Then, at last, we got electricity!

THE FARM KITCHEN

I suppose this was the most essential and important room, where so much went on and where, most days, one lived until tea-time. I suppose ours was quite a modern kitchen at that time (late twenties, early thirties), at least for a farmhouse.

It had that great plus of gravity-fed cold water, and when the range (or stove) was lit in the morning room (or best kitchen) as it was most days, it gave an ample supply of hot water. It was called 'best kitchen' because Mother used to do all the cooking on or in the stove during the week, except on Saturdays, when the cloam (hot brick oven) was used. I have drawn a plan of our kitchen (see opposite), as it used to be, showing some of the furnishings and utensils used. I hope this will help give you a picture of days gone by.

On Saturday, breakfast was cooked as usual over an open fire in the hearth. The cloam oven, at the end of the hearth, was kindled with small faggots (bundles of wood) until the walls were white with heat. When this was achieved, the ash was removed by using an iron scraper, letting the ash fall on the hearth beside and below. It was later carried away to a bin outside, and stored to provide potash for the flower and vegetable garden. Into the oven Mother put a huge dish with a large joint of meat, twenty or so potatoes with three or four chopped onions. A little later, pies of whatever fruits were in season, or large apple dumplings coated in pastry. If you have never tasted a meal cooked in one of these ovens, you have missed a great deal! The taste, compared to modern ovens of today, was of a different class. One can cook the same food in a gas or electric oven of today easily, and with far less effort, but one cannot get that superb flavour and taste that the old cloam oven gave to all its food.

While this was cooking, large pans of home-made bread and yeast-cake were kneaded and left in front of the hearth fire to rise. When the dinner (always called that for farmers' midday meal) was

The Kitchen. (Approx. 22' x 16') ~ As I remember it.

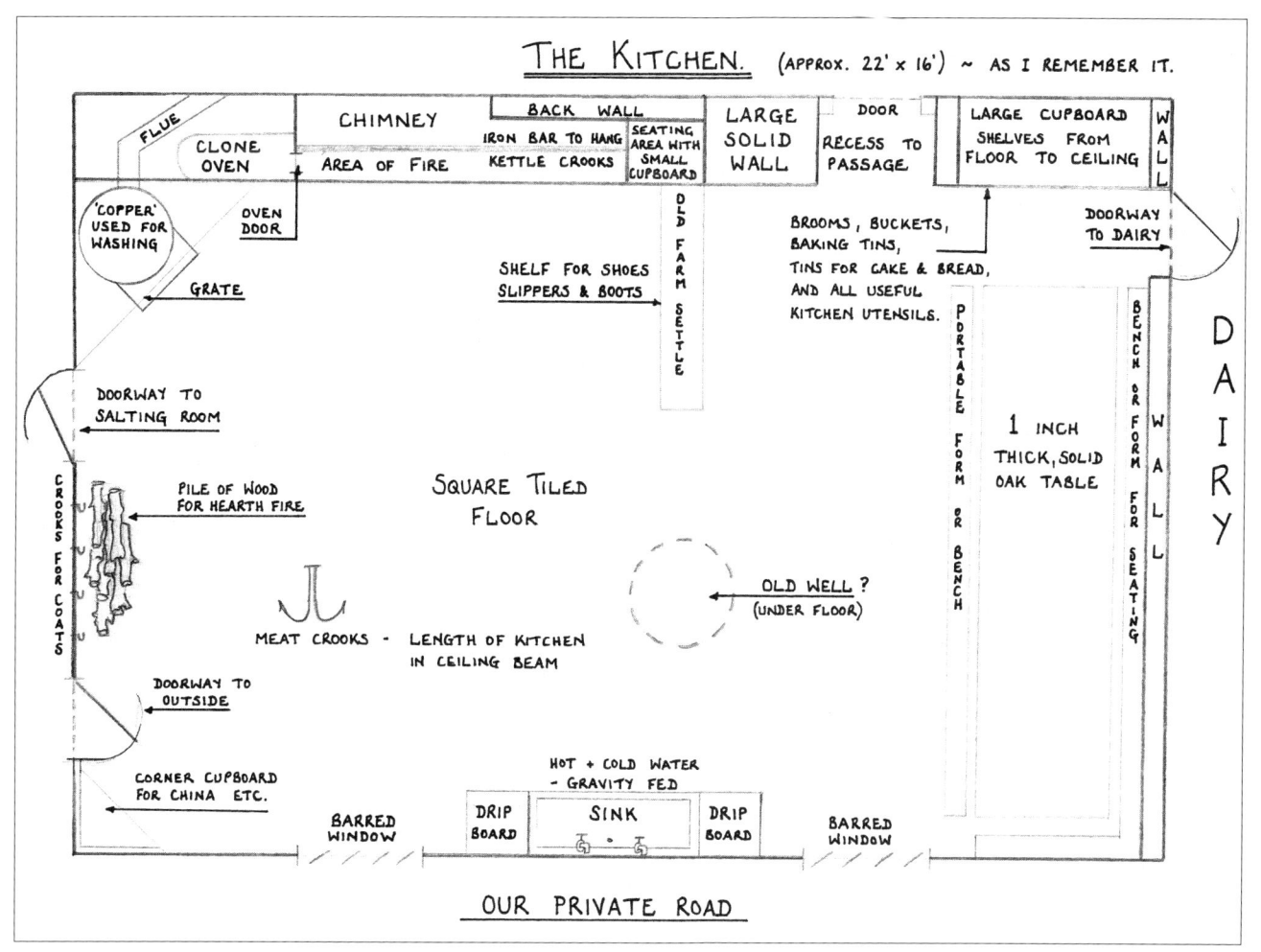

The kitchen at Overton.

taken out, the cakes and bread were put in. So, Saturdays were baking days in the farm kitchens.

Mondays, no matter what the weather, was washing day. A copper (holding about forty or so gallons of water) which stood on its own in the corner of the kitchen, had to be filled with buckets of water, carried there by hand from a tap across the other side of the room. It had its own grate underneath which, like the oven, was fuelled by small bundles of wood. This would be lit at about 7.30am, before breakfast, and the water allowed to heat during the meal. It would usually be boiling by the time we finished breakfast. This would fill the kitchen with steam! Soap, grated, was added (no powder in those days) and the washing for the eight people was put in the boiling water. A bell-shaped plunger, with holes around its rim and fastened to a wooden handle, was used to circulate the water by plunging it up and down amongst the clothes in the copper. This went on for some time and when it was thoroughly clean, was removed and placed in large metal trays with handles each end and carried by two people to a large stone trough (kitchen sink). Here it was rinsed, to remove the soap and dirt. It was then wrung by hand to remove much of the water, then placed into another metal container and taken to the mangle (two rollers between which the sheets or other clothing were put) with someone turning the handle and someone feeding the machine. The rollers were pressed together by a spring which could be either tightened or slackened by turning a screw. The water was squeezed out and was collected in another metal tray which was placed below the mangle.

The clothes-line was some 120 feet long and supported by eight feet high by three inches by three inch wooden posts. The line itself was a length of heavy fencing wire. On numerous occasions I have seen this line full from end to end! On these washing days, the soapy water from the wash was collected and some of it used to scrub the kitchen and dairy floors. The kitchen was a busy, bustling and hard-working place.

The ironing, when tackled sometime later, was done by heating irons in the hearth fire. (As one got cold, you put it back to heat and used another). They were shaped like the modern iron, but had to be placed into a shiny, metal sheaf. They were held there by two spring-clips running each side of the handle and holding it firmly in place. These irons were very hot and had to be handled with great care; never with bare hands.

Another big day in the kitchen was thursdays, when all the vegetables had to be cleaned and the butter and cream packed, ready for market the next day.

When one killed a pig, the kitchen became a butcher's Shop for a day or so! The cleaning of the pig's pots (intestines) - the washing of these took a couple of days. These were then used as skins for the sausages and hogs pudding. The salting of pork and ham took two or three days, rubbing in the salt. The mincing of odd bits of pig (ears, nose, trotters, cheeks and parts of the belly) added to groats, were made into hogs puddings. The pig's pots were filled with this mixture. It was in great demand. It was very tasty, and we could have sold three times as much to customers of many years standing. In fact, it had to be rationed to make sure it went round!

Over the open fire, which rarely went out, was a bar some four feet above, running the full length of the hearth. On the bar were three or four adjustable crooks (see page 16). By simply lifting a ratchet, you could easily lengthen or shorten the crooks. On one crook there was always a large case-iron kettle holding at least two gallons of water. It was kept quite high when not needed, but still kept pretty warm. When boiling water was needed, it was lowered and quickly brought to the boil. On the others were:- saucepan with metal handles and a lid and a couple of crocks which could be used for boiling potatoes, greens, etc. All the fires and grates were fuelled by wood from the farm, so quite a time was spent each year making sure we did not run short.

Bellows, hand made, were an essential part of the kitchen equipment. If the hearth fire had died down, a few sticks from the faggot pile in the kitchen and some long puffs from the Bellows, would soon put things right. The fire would burst into bright flame and the kettle would soon be boiling again.

THE DAIRY

This was next to the kitchen and was another important room in the farmhouse, where work went on every day. The tools used in a dairy were:- separator, churn and butter maker.

The separator was a machine used to separate the cream from the milk. It was done by allowing milk to flow over fast-spinning cups, about twenty-six in all. By doing this, the cream (which was the heaviest part of the milk) was separated by remaining nearest to the spinning cups or plates,

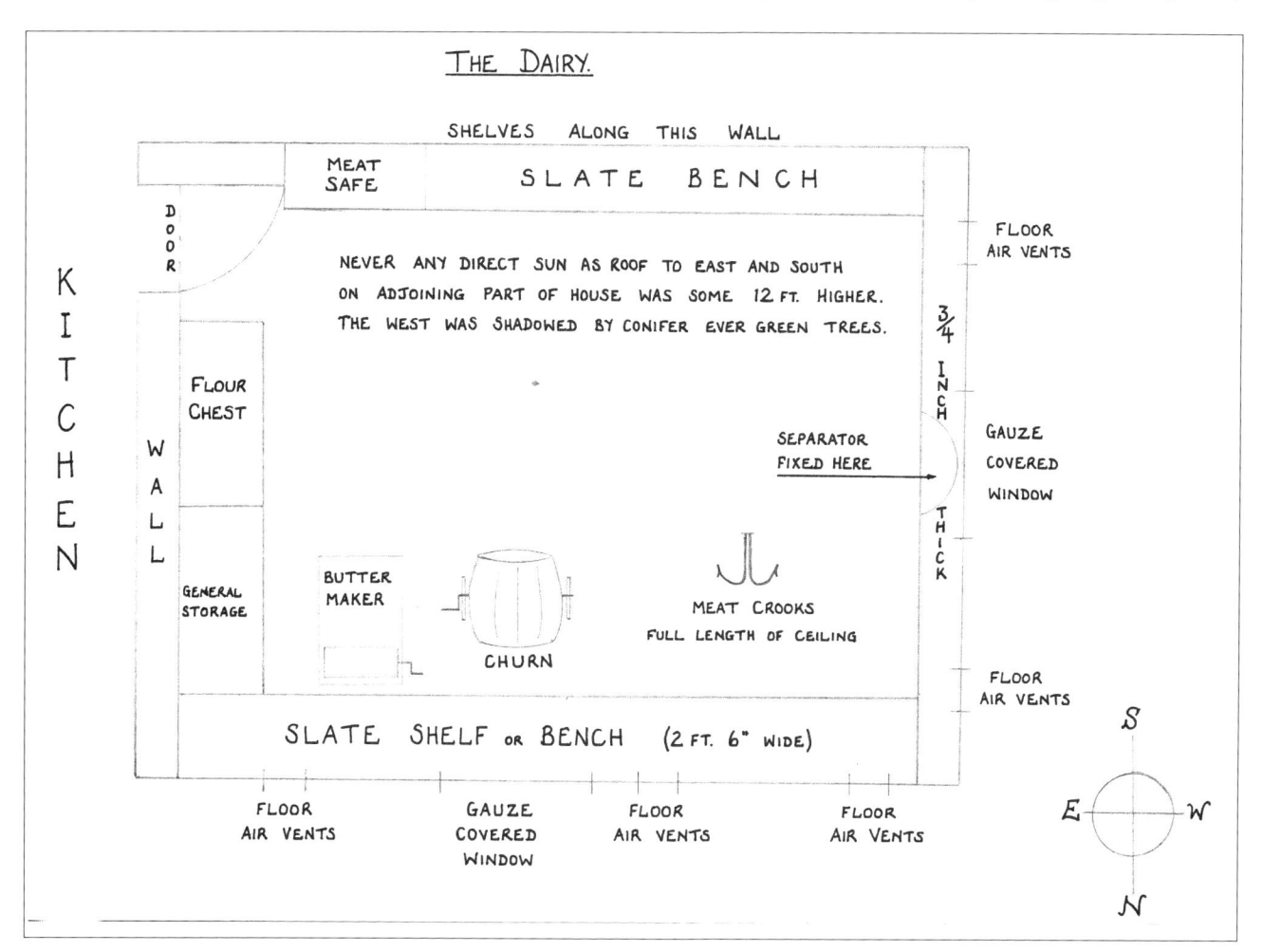

THE DAIRY.

SHELVES ALONG THIS WALL

MEAT SAFE — SLATE BENCH

KITCHEN WALL

DOOR

FLOOR AIR VENTS

NEVER ANY DIRECT SUN AS ROOF TO EAST AND SOUTH ON ADJOINING PART OF HOUSE WAS SOME 12 FT. HIGHER. THE WEST WAS SHADOWED BY CONIFER EVER GREEN TREES.

FLOUR CHEST

3/4 INCH THICK

SEPARATOR FIXED HERE →

GAUZE COVERED WINDOW

GENERAL STORAGE

BUTTER MAKER

CHURN

MEAT CROOKS FULL LENGTH OF CEILING

FLOOR AIR VENTS

SLATE SHELF or BENCH (2 FT. 6" WIDE)

FLOOR AIR VENTS — GAUZE COVERED WINDOW — FLOOR AIR VENTS — FLOOR AIR VENTS

S / E — W / N

and the remainder (the lighter part of the milk) was thrown farther away. These were collected, using two different spouts from the separator, into different containers.

This machine was used each day after morning milking. About four gallons of milk was processed this way, daily. The cream was used for meals and making butter. The skimmed milk being used for feeding calves and pigs. At first, it was done by turning the handle about ten mimutes each time but, much later, a small petrol engine was installed. The exhaust was piped through a hole in the wall to the outside. Not very hygienic but very effective. No one was poisoned and no one had any tummy troubles!

The skimmed milk fed to the calves was at first warmed, to blood heat, taken and then mixed with milk direct from the cows, in tin buckets to the Yard. You placed your fingers in the calf's mouth, and when he or she started to suck your fingers (thinking they were their mother's teat) you gently raised the bucket with your free hand and moved the hand in the calf's mouth slowly, into the bucket of milk. If lucky the calf would keep sucking away and the milk would enter their mouth in the gaps between your fingers. This method did not always work and sometimes it took days. If that was the case, the calf had to be fed by bottle, putting the neck of the bottle in its mouth and gently pouring the milk down its throat. Any surplus milk was fed to the pigs.

The cream was left in large enamel-covered pans. It was used for meals, twice daily, on sweets, pies, puddings, etc., at midday, and on bread and jam for tea. For our supper, we three children each had our own bowl of junket, a milk dish - milk with rennet added, which turned the milk into a semi-solid state, something like jelly or custard. We used to add sugar and about a quarter of an inch of cream over the top. It was delicious.

Every two days in the summer, the remainder of the cream was put in a churn and churned into butter. The hotter the weather, the longer it took. An average time of a quarter of an hour of steady churning would do the trick. Again, the churn was turned by hand but later again by petrol engine. The churn, with wooden beaters on the inside, was turned over and over on a wooden frame, mixing and banging the cream until it was a fairly solid mass, and now butter. Any surplus milk left by the separator was poured away, by removing a bung in the end of the churn and perhaps as much as a pint would be removed from the cream. This was known as butter-milk and fed to the pigs.

The butter was then removed from the churn into a wooden frame with notched roller. Some salt was added and then 'rolled' and 'worked' into the butter, then weighed into half-pound or pound slabs. It was then taken between two wooden butter bats and patted into the cube shape required. It was now ready for the market and the many customers from the village of Bishops Tawton, half a mile away down the hill.

BUTTER WORKER.

Along one wall was a huge wooden chest with a lid. This was used to store flour, which was bought by the sack full (l.5 hundredweight). It did not last long in those days.

The fats we ate (solid fat bacon, very fat meat, pastry and puddings, lots of cream and butter, cheese, fresh milk) by today's thinking, were all the wrong and harmful foods, yet most country folk lived to ripe old ages! So much for your modern food charts - very few died of heart trouble.

This, I hope, has given you an insight into the ways of transport and the life and goings on in many farm houses at that time. The low wages, long hours, big families and yet people were content, happy and mostly honest. There seemed plenty of time to do things in a leisurely manner, not the mad rush and bustle of today. You had to make your own fun and pleasure, not sit back and press a button for the TV, when conversation ceases and all eyes are on the 'box'. Silence reigns - progress? I suppose so, but at what cost? Great changes have taken place during the last Seventy years, probably greater changes than at any time in history, especially on the farms. I will try and deal with these in the chapters to come in this book. The ones that have affected one and all working on the land.

MEMORIES OF OVERTON

Outside there was always a wood-rick (small brushwood tied in bundles) or two in the yard, and piles of poles, old apple trees, trees blown down by winter gales. Somehow we managed to find enough fire-wood for our needs.

Overton was sheltered from the north and east by Codden Hill, some 660 feet high, but wide open to the West and South, with magnificent views of the Taw Valley.

Overton - our 'little grey home in the west'.

The woods and church of Tawstock, and on clear days, Dartmoor, could be seen some forty miles distant. Yes, a perfect 'little grey home in the west'.

I have many memories of the sixty-nine years I lived there. The people of the past; the workers, the stock (sheep, cattle, horses, pigs and dogs). Of Quaddy the clum ewe that produced six sets of quads, two sets of triplets and a total of thirty lambs. She died on the farm of old age - what a great ewe and mum!

I recall the day a fore-horse bolted (a horse in front of the horse, in shafts pulling heavy loads up hill). The horse in shafts was thrown to the ground and came to rest on the road, on his knees. He was then dragged some 100 yards down the road. There was no flesh left on the knee-joints, so he had to be put down.

Then there was a Devon Bull found dead in his pen. A post-mortem revealed a bristle, from a broom, had somehow punctured his heart.

And I remember the last horse retired on the farm, after twenty years service. A man came to ask if he could buy the horse, to make up a load to send to the Continent for meat. He offered me a good price, over £200, a lot of money in the early sixties. I told him he was not for sale. He had been a great servant to the Farm and would enjoy his remaining days there. The next morning the horse was stretched out in the field, dead. I'm glad I did not sell him.

And then there was Landy, the landacre gilt, which I had purchased in pig and who produced four mummified pigs. Not much return for the £300 which I paid for her. But then all these mishaps occur. That's farming!

And I recall the pride Father and I felt with a field of corn, on which I had done all the work ploughing, working down, and tilling with Dad. On the drill cutting with the Binder, helping with carting ricking in the field and finally threshing it, yielding a remarkable 102 bushels per acre - a record crop for those days.

The came the time when the steam engine brought the thresher to the Farm.

THRESHING DAYS

On threshing days the contractor would arrive at the farm at about 6.30am, light the boiler in the engine to get up steam for 8.45am, when threshing would start. Having lit the fire, they would come into the kitchen where a fried breakfast would be provided - fat bacon, eggs, potatoes, bread and butter and hot, sweet or unsweet tea. It took nine to twelve men to form a threshing team. Two to pitch corn from ricks, two men on top of the threshers (one to cut the cord binding the sheaves and one to feed into the thresher), one or two men to look after the bags which filled with corn and had to be carted off to store or granary. One man to take the straw from the trusser, or maybe two if it had to be taken any distance. One to remove chaff and dust. One to keep steam up and look after the engine. How our lungs stuck the foul, air I shall never know.

When the threshers came to your area, you lent men to farms for a days threshing, and when the thresher came to you, you had theirs back to help you. Thus, many a farm-hand spent four or five days in one week threshing at his place of work or helping out on neighbouring farms. How sweet was the smell of steam and smoke. How good the sound of the steam engine, gently cuffing away and the low and soft hum of the threshing machine.

The fun we had as youths, killing some of the hundreds of mice and often up to a hundrd rats!

Lunchtime during threshing at the author's wife's home.

Hard work: reed combing on a North Devon farm in the 1920s.

At ten o'clock, a break of some twenty minutes, was taken. A tin kettle full of tea (about two gallons), mugs and cups of all shapes and sizes. A huge market basket full of cooked or baked food. Yeast cake (well buttered), bread and cheese were always there, sometimes home-made sausage rolls. The men never washed but ate the food, dust, muck and all with great zest. Most of them lived to a ripe old age; so much for hygiene!

At one o'clock, they came into the house to a baked meal. Beef, potatoes, sprouts, swede, turnip or cabbage, whatever was in season. Followed by apple pie and cream and tea. Usually, at about three-thirty to four o'clock, the threshing would cease and the contractor would move on to the next farm. If it was too late and near darkness, they would have to leave it until the next morning. The boiler would be lit well before dawn, so that when the first light of dawn arrived they were ready for the road.

Threshing meant busy days for all concerned. The ladies had much to do, providing and serving meals for ten or twelve men.

For the men to look after the stock and help with the threshing during the day, meant getting up extra early to do the daily chores, i.e. milking, feeding all cattle and sheep, mucking out and bedding down. The same applied when the days threshing ended. Work often went on to eight o'clock or beyond.

The work in the fields at harvest, although helped by various machines, the hard work of pitching and carting and rick-making, was done by human effort. How good it was to know that as the winter storms broke and snow and hail fell, that the barns were full of hard-gained fodder and that the cattle were snug and warm in the yards. A feeling of great satisfaction.

CHAPTER FOUR
THE THIRTIES

In the early Thirties my sister went to Guys Hospital, London, to see if anything could be done to help her walk again. She spent some four months there, having operations and medical treatment. Then home for a short spell, then back again for more treatment and operations. After another month she came home for good, and with the aid of two sticks and heavy callipers on both legs, was able to walk a few steps. We were all delighted that at last she could walk, though only for short distances. By the end of the year she was able to walk from room to room - a great improvement. To go up the stairs she would sit on the bottom stair and, using her arms, put her hands on the next stair above and lift her body by straightening her arms and shuffling her bottom up one stair. Then repeat the same process all over again. There were sixteen stairs, so it was an exhausting operation. She seemed to have extra strength in her arms to make up for her useless legs. She gradually improved a bit more and, with special adaptions, learned to drive a small car. What a joy that must have been for her, to expand what had been a very limited life. She is now nearly eighty years old and although chair and bed bound, is still bright and cheerful. No complaining, just plodding on. She drove for about fifty years and never had an accident - not a bad record for a badly disabled person.

About 1936 my father spoke to the Electricity Company at Barnstaple, asking if it was possible to bring electricity to Bishops Tawton. They told him that they could do so if they had enough people, or houses, which would use their power, to make it worthwhile.

So father decided to canvass the whole village to find out. You would think that everyone would have jumped at the chance. No so! He had to canvass and re-canvass to get enough people to have electricity installed. A few said they could not find the money, perhaps rightly so, but many refused to change their ways and were really afraid of electric current and therefore said no. In the end it made no difference, as just enough people agreed and Bishops Tawton was at last lit by electricity. To bring it to our farm, some half a mile from the village, we had to guarantee to pay £50 a year, for five years. What a bargain! What a change in the yards. No more oil lanterns - just press the switch and all was lit up. Dad had the four cottages, belonging to the farm, wired for electricity - only one or two made use of it. The other two preferred their oil lamps and coal and wood fuel for the old ranges, for cooking. It was quite a few years before they changed their minds!

Indoors the range, in the best kitchen, was taken out and a fire-place, with a back boiler, took its place. A new electric cooker was installed in the kitchen. The cloam oven was now barely used. Electric cleaners replaced the dust-pan and brush. The radio now ran off the mains - the days of the wet batteries now over. No more cleaning oil lamps and no more candle-sticks!

Small electric machines to drive the sheep clippers. Life indoors and out was far easier now we had the mains, thanks to Dad's hard work.

Nothing of great interest occurred during the early thirties (my school days). The highlights and days of joy were not too plentiful. One thing we used to look forward to was Barnstaple Fair. Three days in mid September. The beautiful steam engines in all their glory. Their shining brass on ornate fittings. A really great sight, standing there softly puffing away, supplying the power to drive the dynamo, which supplied all the power and lighting for the whole fairground.

The cheap-jacks, the small side-shows. The boxing booths, where local lads could challenge the boxers from the fair booth, and if still on their feet after three rounds, received the princely sum of ten shillings.

The galloping horses, the swings, the helter-skelter (a high tower with a shoot on the outside, running around the tower to the ground below. You had a door-mat on which you sat and slid down from the top. Wall of death - motor-bikes ridden around the inside of a huge wooden cylinder. Ghost train, penny slot-machines, Noah's ark - a switch-back, roundabout rides, and, in the late thirties, the bumper cars.

The price, in those days, was two (old) pence a ride in the early thirties, rising to six (old) pence in the late thirties. So, if you went to the fair with one pound in your pocket, you could ride on all the different rides and visit all the side-shows and still have money for the coconut shy, darts, etc.

LEISURE

My brother and I belonged to the Boy Scouts. The highlight of the year being a fortnight's camp at Croyde Bay. Many of the Scouts came from children's Homes, and those fourteen days of freedom and fun (cricket and football on the beach, swimming in the sea, fishing from the rocks, camp songs around the fire at night) must have been another world to them. A fortnight away from all the coldness and discipline of the children's home to freedom and friendship of those days at Croyde. We all enjoyed these camps and made many friends.

During the Christmas holidays, my brother and I spent a great deal of the time catching moles - skinning same and nailing the skins on boards to dry. We used about twenty traps, which we tilled in mole-runs in fields. The moles came along and pushed the tiller, which kept the jaws apart allowing the two halves to snap together, clasping the mole in its grasp, and in a very short time it would be dead. Perhaps we would catch 150 moles during a three-week period. We would then send the skins to a firm in Lincolnshire, and wait for a Postal Order to arrive, with the cash for three weeks work. If they were a good lot of skins, we may get three pounds, if not so good, about two pounds. No much for all the time and labour. About two (old) pence an hour! But we had cleared the fields of moles for another year.

My brother and I played a few pranks during the thirties.

One night, near Christmas, knowing the carol-singers were coming, we decided to give them a wet welcome. We placed a bucket of water on a low wall, by the entrance gate (hidden by a gate post), so that when the gate was opened the bucket (attached by string to the gate) would be pulled and over would go the water, drenching someone's feet. We were not very popular with carol-singers, that night.

On another occasion, after a day's threshing, we caught several mice by their tails, put them in tins and took them to chapel. We were hoping to release them and get them to where the girls were sitting. We let them out on the floor, but instead of going to where the girls were sitting, climbed up the end of our seat and ran up and down behind us. A man sitting behind us spotted them, and quickly killed them using his hymn book. We said that we had been threshing all day and that the mice must have got into our pockets, unknown to us.

On another occasion, while playing cricket, I hit a ball too hard and it went through the conservatory roof, smashing a large pain of glass, near the cob and stone wall of the farmhouse. If we broke glass, we had to pay for it! We had a bright idea. We found a stone, not too big, and put it under the hole on the conservatory floor. We found a bit of cob dust and sprinkled it on the floor around the stone - and said nothing. The next morning Mum discovered the stone and the hole in the roof. She said to Dad, 'There must be a rat in the roof, it has dug a stone out of the top of the wall and broken a pane of glass. Something should be done about it'. We said nothing and did not pay for the glass.

On another occasion my brother and I, with two other Scouts, went to camp at Croyde. We borrowed one of their bell tents and took food for a week.

We dug latrines for the whole camp for the following week. A cow was kept in the field where we were camping. It was very quiet and docile. So, with the aid of a tin jug, I used to milk about a pint each night, after dark. We had free milk for a week.

A master at my school had a mole, or moles, in his garden. He asked me if I could catch it, or them, for him. He would give me sixpence for each mole caught. I soon caught the mole, but thought, 'There's money to be made here'. I took the same mole along for the next three days, making out it was another mole. In that way I earned two shillings. He was so pleased that he actually gave me two shillings and sixpence!

A SAD DAY

Perhaps the saddest blow of those years was the death of Annie, my second mum. It was a terrible loss to me. She had always been there. Someone I could always turn to. Like my real mum, she will never be forgotten. On the day of the funeral something strange happened to me. (I was 14 years old). I was standing at her grave-side and somehow got parted from my family. I was quite alone, ready to burst into tears, when I felt a hand on my shoulder which gave a calming effect, and helped keep my emotions back. I turned to see who it was, but there was no-one within ten feet of me. Then I knew Annie was at rest. I felt at peace, knowing that somewhere, someone cared

SUNDAYS IN THE THIRTIES

On Sundays we only did what had to be done, on the farm. Milking, feeding and caring of the stock. Most of the people went to church or chapel at least once, and many went twice. I can well remember both chapel and church full on many occasions. On anniversaries and harvest festivals, it was over-flowing. On chapel anniversaries, which were held in May, it was great to see the ladies and girls in all their finery. Their new hats usually gaily decorated with either fruits or flowers and highly coloured with ribbons or feathers. The younger girls had pretty new dresses, socks and shoes. It was like a miniature Manequin Parade.

We never knew what to expect. It gave the ladies a chance to ask, 'What do you think', of someone's hat, or someone's dress - some of which were pretty outrageous. The 'Mrs Buckets' of yester-year. Then the harvest festival, when the chapels and churches were so beautiful. In fact, they became a show gound for the fruits of the year. Everyone brought their best to put on show. The church windows, aisles, choir stalls and even the altars were bedecked with flowers and fruits of the year. The sheaves of corn, wheat, oats and barley; the huge vegetables, marrows and pumpkins. The rosy, red apples, the pears, tomatoes, beans, huge onions, large bunches of grapes and the choice root vegetables; beetroot, carrots, potatoes and parsnips - a glorious sight was there for all to see, and the scent for all to smell.

Everyone, from the smallest cottage or the largest country house, gave their best. The farmers, with their corn and dairy products, gave thanks for a good harvest and for the weather - rain and sunshine was so essential to the farmer and his crops. The harvest festivities were a feature of the year. How good it was to sing the words of that great harvest hymn, 'All Is Safely Gathered In Ere The Winter Storms Begin'. The hard work in the fields was now complete, and the barns were full. Come what may, gales, rain, sleet or snow there was enough fodder for the harshest of winters. Nature would sleep for a while, but would burst again into life and vigour in the spring, when the cycle would start all over again.

I suppose I am some sort of Christian. I believe in something beyond the grave, though what, I am not sure. If there was nothing, then life would be pointless. If there is not a supreme power, how did our universe come into being? Scientists can say that millions of years ago Man emerged as some strange creature, from the sea, and over millions of years gradually became what we are today. Maybe that is correct, maybe not. But, if correct, where did the sea and where did the strange creatures come from? Something or somebody had to start it all. I am sure there is some supreme being - some sort of life after death. Remember the hand on my shoulder at Annie's funeral, when there was no-one there? Why did St Paul's, during the war, stand untouched when all around lay in ruins? Was someone trying to tell us something? I don't know, but somehow I feel that the message was that there was something far stronger than bombs, or anything that Man could make or do. Perhaps it was just luck - somehow I think not!

LEAVING SCHOOL

In l937 I felt that as I was not very accademic at school, I could spend my time far better in starting a career outside. I talked this over with Dad. He said that he was not too happy with me leaving school, without achieving the same standards as my brother, but he did see my point of view. What did I want to do as a career? I don't think he particularly wanted me home on the farm, as my brother was already there, an heir to carry on the farming tradition of both sides of the family. He never said so in words, but I felt that that was what he was thinking.

When I told him I thought I would like to try my luck in the acting and musical world, I don't think he was very impressed. He suggested many other careers, i.e. auctioneer, veterinary surgeon and agricultural engineering and, if not certain, to spend two years on the farm. If I still wanted to try my luck in the entertainment world, he would pay my fees for drama and music school.

That is what we decided I should do. A fair and just compromise. I was only sixteen, and would be only eighteen years old in two years time. So, home on the farm I came, in September, 1937.

Having left school in July, I started my farming career in August, 1937, age sixteen years. I told my Father I wanted no favours and wished to learn to do every job on the farm. In other words, to muck in and do the same sort of work as the other workers. Even if I should later seek a career in the entertainment world (with this in mind I kept my voice in trim by joining the male voice choir and still had my lessons from Richard Russel. I sang at various concerts and took small acting parts in plays and sketches), I would not have wasted my time. I would have a sound and basic grasp of farming, its ways and needs, and still be able to do reasonably well with the many and varied jobs on the farm at the time. I say varied, because most farms were of the mixed type - beef or milk; sheep potatoes, swede, turnips, corn, sugar-beet, poultry and a few pigs. The feeling at that time was that, if one of these failed, another would succeed. Although one would never make a fortune, farming in this manner, you would seldom go bankrupt. 'Never put all your eggs in one basket', was the yardstick on many farms. How right they were for the small, mixed farms of North Devon.

Barnstaple Male Voice Choir. The author is in the back row, second from left.

DAD'S WAY OF FARMING AND ITS WORK

I suppose Dad's farm could be described as mixed beef. It included a herd of Devons (Ruby Reds). and a flock of closewool Ewes, some kept pure for replacing breeding stock. They were often crossed with Dorset Down or Suffolk, for fat lamb production. About twenty-five to thirty acres of corn was grown. One field of wheat was sold for cash, the grain sent to the millers and the reed used for thatching. Roots grown included five acres of mangolds for cattle, in the winter. A field of swedes or turnips for feeding the sheep and, if the price was good, for human consumption. During the war years, four or five acres of potatoes were grown. A couple of sows were kept to make use of kitchen waste and any surplus, separated milk. A few hens of various breeds were kept in the top yard and fed on home-grown corn, and what they could find about the yard. In fact, 'free-range' hens in the true sense.

Butter, cream, apples and vegetables were provided from the large kitchen garden, were sold either to shops or on the stall in the Barnstaple Pannier Market. The main fodder was hay, very little silage in those days.

These were the stocking and cropping policies carried out on many Devon farms, in the late thirties. The staff were two full-time men, father, my brother and myself. Casual labour was brought in for harvesting hay and corn, and on threshing days. We kept three horses and a light cob, which served a dual purpose - to do light work on the farm and could also be used to ride around the farm, to see the stock daily. An old Blackstone engine, single piston, was kept to drive the farm machinery, i.e. thresher, roller mill, chaff cutter and mangel pulper and circular saw. Most farms had one of these engines at that time.

The thresher was a smaller model of the machine we used to hire (and thresh direct from the Dutch barn) was stationary. The corn had to be loaded on the cart, taken from the Dutch barn and put in small ricks beside the thresher, ready for threshing - a rather laborious way of doing things.

The roller mill was used for preparing corn for the cattle and sheep. It consisted of two metal wheels with flat surfaces, about nine inches wide. These could be controlled by a screw which put pressure on the rollers (wheels) to the correct degree, to break and flatten the corn. That was fed from the hutch above, to a gap above the rollers, passed through, crushed and deposited on the barn floor.

The chaff cutter was a machine with knives attached to its spokes. These flew around at great speed, chopping corn or straw fed into it from a wooden chute, with a safety guard at the end to protect one's hands. The end result being that, anything passing through was chopped into pieces, about two inches in length. This was usually fed to the horses, mixed with corn.

The mangel pulper was a large, flat metal disc with shart rounded holes, which stood off some half an inch from the flat surface, thus cutting pieces out of the mangels and dropping them on the floor below. These were about the size and shape of potato chips.

The binder: the mechanism of the binder was driven from the land wheel, about one foot six inches wide, with cleat on the surface to avoid slipping. This was connected by chains and sprockets, cog-wheels, to other moving parts. The binder, used for cutting corn, was a vast improvement on the old reaper, as it not only cut the corn but tied it up in neat sheaves, before depositing it on the ground.

The corn was cut by about twenty-four blades, moving too and fro between metal toes, thus trapping the corn against the toes. These blades were roughly the shape of one side of a pyramid.

When the corn had been cut a wooden reel, rotating towards the binder, helped the corn to a canvas, revolving on two rollers. This took the corn to the right-hand side of the binder, where two more canvases, on rollers, trapped the corn in between their rollers (with the aid of battens riveted on the canvas) which carried it to the packers (curved metal arms on a bar). When it had packed corn, the packers would disappear below the packing area, allowing more corn to arrive from the canvases. The action was then repeated again.

A huge needle, threaded with binder cord, took this cord to the knotter, where it was tied by a revolving movement. The jaws of the knotter opening and shutting. Opening to grab the cord from the needle and shutting to tie the knot.

Three more metal arms, on a rotating bar, then deposited the tied corn sheafs.

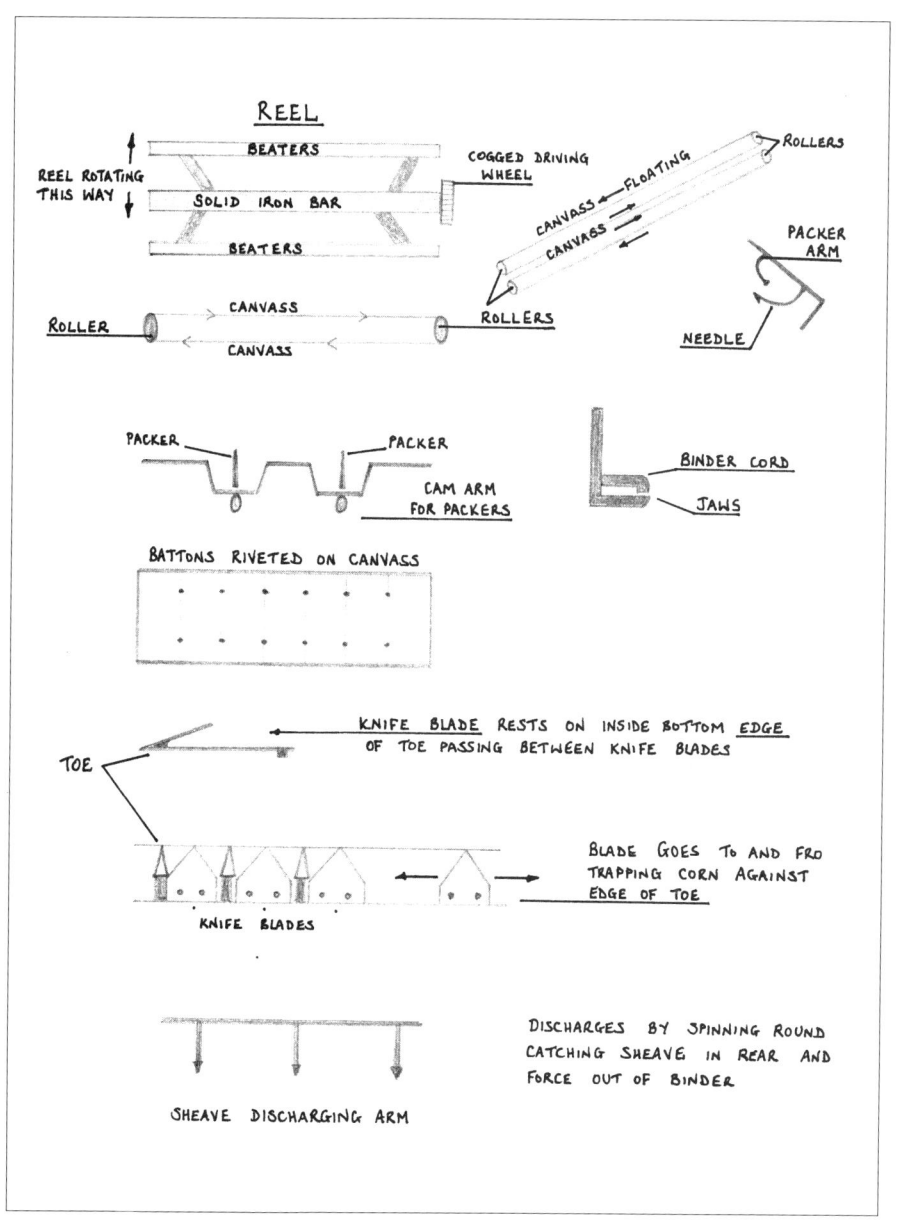

The workings of the binder.

NOVEMBER 1943

Perhaps I should now attempt to try to tell you how the work went during the year. The various types of work, the rota in which they were done. At the beginning of August, when I started work on the farm, my first job was to assist with the sheep dipping. Sheep were penned, two men did the catching and pushing into the dip (a bath some 3ft. wide, 12ft. in length and some 5ft. at the deep end) with steps leading out at the far end to the drying pen where sheep were allowed to drain, the dip returning by gravity to the sheep bath. A man stood on the side of the dip with a small pole with two bits sticking out, one each side. His job was to push the sheep completely under and to turn, if necessary, to allow them to escape at the far end.

The dip, containing arsenic, was very good at killing the ticks (bloodsucking insects) about the size of a ladybird, but useless against the blow-fly. It was much later into the 1950s when an effective dip was produced against that pest.

The dipping went on for three or four days. After we had dipped our sheep, some 400 to 450, our neighbouring farmers were allowed to bring their sheep and use our yards and dip, for which they paid us the princely sum of 3 pence or 4 pence a sheep. That included the price of the dip.

It was now time to start the corn harvest, often a long drawn affair if the weather was showery or wet. The corn was cut with a binder, which cut and deposited the corn in sheaves on the ground, about 20 inches in circumference, tied with binder cord around the middle. These were then picked

My Father and brother (right) at Devon County Show with two prize ram lambs.

up by other farm hands and put in stacks (two sheaves placed at an angle against each other) or stooks, containing 6 or 8 sheaves. Each stook was left to dry for 10 to 14 days - so we prayed for fine weather. These stacks (or stooks) were in straight rows and looked a treat in the evening sun when shadows spread across the fields.

The binder - was pulled by either two or three horses - hot and tiring work on a hot day. When the corn was thought to be dry it was carted to the Dutch barn in the farmyard, ready for the thresher later in the year. Three horses and three carts were used to carry out this job. Two men in the field loading one cart, one man (usually me) whose duty was to take the empty cart to the field and return with a full one. Two men in the yard, one unloading the cart (pitching) and one making ricks. Using this system, some 6 acres of corn could be cleared daily. If the stooks were soaked by heavy rain, it was a different matter. The sheaves would have to be turned inside out to dry. This was done by placing two thumbs into the centre of

Evening shadows on a cornfield with rows of stooks.

the sheaves and rotating each hand in opposite direction, thus turning the sheaves inside out. This was very time consuming but often the only way to get the corn dry. If the stubble contained any weeds, this was worked out with either a scuffle, or very shallow ploughing. The bate, as weed was called, was burnt - a laboursome and tedious job!

Farmyard manure stored in the yards during the summer was now carted to the field in horse-drawn butts - a cart on two wheels (see opposite for photo of butt) with a trip stick which when removed, allowed the butt to rise at the front end and drop at the back, depositing the load on the ground. The load was too big to put into one heap, so part had to be forked out by hand. Perhaps three or four heaps per load in heaps about 12 to 15 feet apart. When the field had been covered in this manner, we were sent with forks to spread it evenly over the field for winter ploughing. A hardworking and back-breaking job. This was one of the least sought-after jobs on the farm but had to be done.

It is now September, the time to start picking the apples in an orchard of some 1.5 acres. This too was a time-consuming job, and took two or three men about two weeks to complete. They were picked, carted and stored in the apple room on shelves and in hutches. I suppose somewhere in the region of 4.5 tons would be roughly the weight harvested. The varieties included bramleys, blenheim long bider, Effingham pippin, thin skin sweet-cleave, and cornish jelly flower. I do remember the beautiful smell which greeted you when you opened the door and entered the apple room.

These apples were sold by Mum in the market, a few to shops but a lot to customers in the Brendon area on Exmoor. No apples were grown there, so we had a very good round. They used to be taken in a large trailer towed behind our car - half a ton to 15 cwt. at a time.

Now it was potato time. We did not grow many at this time, enough for ourselves and perhaps a few spare, so they were dug by hand - a couple of day's work for one man.

The rams were put in with the ewes in early August and had now completed their job for the year! The lambing should start by about the 1st January.

Hedge-trimming by hand and topping was being done in between essential jobs.

The last crop to harvest were the five acres of mangels. This took all hands (except Dad) about a week to complete. One or two men pulling and taking off leaves, leaving mangels in neat rows. One man loading and carting to cave in the yard. Very hard and backaching job, as he had to pick the mangels from the ground with his hands and throw them into the butt which now had inflated rubber tyres! The carters would get help from the pullers at times. What a job in wet weather. The field then became a quagmire, mud stuck to everything - horses hooves, your farm boots and the wheels of the butt and worst of all, the mangels. They were easily unloaded, by removing the trip-stick, tipping the butt and depositing the load on the floor. This was the last big job of the year. Much time would be spent in tidying up hedges, casting tons of earth with shovels or forks, layering the tops to form a solid low fence. To cut off larger wood on hedges for firewood for winter. Cutting up any trees blown down by winter gales. Removing any dead or blown down apple trees and sawing up same with circular saw and storing in log shed adjoining the farmhouse.

Loading mangels into a butt cart - just as the author remembers this arduous task.

In mid October, depending on the weather, much time was spent in feeding the 100 or so head of cattle. Mucking out, bedding up, milking by hand four or five gallons for household use, carting hay from sheds to lofts for feeding, bringing in mangels from clamps to store in the yard. Cleaning water gullies around many hedges. Mending and repairing farm gates, renewing gate posts where needed; in fact, giving the farm outside a real spring-clean.

George, the horseman, and his team of horses would plough first for the winter wheat and work down and till the same. In a good days ploughing he would plough about an acre and walk about 14 miles doing it. He also had to take out cattle dung and dump it on pasture land, where it was spread again by hand. Then there were the threshing days, already explained in previous chapters. We found plenty of jobs to do, though life was a bit easier than in the harvest seasons.

My brother and I used to spend a couple of short days (from 10am-3.30pm) after morning feeding and before evening feeding of stock and rabbiting. We used a ferret and nets and guns, and were responsible for keeping the rabbit population in check. We were never overrun by rabbits and I

The end of a day's ploughing.

suppose that during the months of November and December we would kill somewhere between 450 and 500 on a farm of nearly 200 acres. So you can tell by these figures we did a really good job. We were allowed to keep the money received from the sale of the rabbits, only 6 pence to 10 pence per head, so we did not make a fortune. Still, it was quite fun and a change from working on the farm.

After Christmas the lambing season began. We used to lamb down about 300 ewes. We had some off ground at Georgeham and rented 40 acres at Bittadon. Both these places were about 12 miles distant. We used to walk ewes there in mid-September, doing the journeys in two days, putting them up for a rest half-way on farms along the route, for which we paid a small fee.

We brought them home in early December, a month before lambing was due to start, to feed them with corn about a fortnight before lambing, to build up their milk and to protect against Twin disease. There was not a great deal of traffic on the roads in those days, but I still hated the job. It took about four hours each day to complete the journey.

The lambing, in those days, was done out of doors in a couple of small fields and a 1.5 acre orchard - not too bad in dry weather but sometimes on bad and wet and bitterly cold nights, the results were near disaster! My brother used to stay up late at night and, if quiet, would go to bed at about 3 or 4 o'clock. I used to get up at about 6.30am in the morning, thus we covered most of the 24 hours of the day. I suppose that if we finished the lambing season with 400 lambs, we had done pretty well. And if we had lost 10 to 15 ewes we had not done too badly. We had none of the modern drugs in those days - no penicillin and M.B., no lambing in nice, warm quarters indoors like we do today. I don't know why no one lambed indoors, perhaps they thought it unhealthy.

The early lambs were put on the best pastures and creep-fed with lamb nuts bought from the merchants. This pushed on their growth rate, as top prices were usually for Easter lamb, around 37 shillings and 6 pence perhaps, so every one strived to make the early market.

Lambing and odd jobs filled the month of January on the farm. In February, with the first signs of Spring, the horse-man started the spring ploughing, 20 acres or so. Three weeks work. Hay and Swedes were fed to the sheep and all the work for stock, done daily. A day a week was spent in grinding corn for cattle and sheep and cutting chaff for horses; pulping mangels for farm cattle which was then carted around to their stalls in large wooden buckets (mauns), daily. This took quite a time each day.

We all looked forward to the time in April when the grass in the fields would have grown, and the cattle would be turned out to forage for themselves. What a relief!

In March, the horse-man was busy either finishing the ploughing and then working down and planting corn and carting fodder around yards, bringing in and ricking any faggots left in the fields from winter cutting and building wood ricks in the yard.

Spring at last! The sheep had to be 'docked' (the messy wool around their back-passage shorn off) to keep the udder clean and later to help prevent flies from blowing and laying their eggs in the filthy wool. This was a dirty and undesirable job.

After planting the corn, the large vegetable garden was forked or ploughed (nearly half an acre) and then worked down by horse or hand and planted into potatoes, beans, peas, parsnips, carrots, beetroot, onions and green plants for re-planting later.

Then a field would be ploughed, usually a grass field - this would be worked down and planted to mangels in late April or early May. These usually took about a week or ten days to appear and when big enough, the whole staff had to spend all the time available thinning and hoeing weeds. The ground between the rows was done with a horse-drawn machine (called a horse-hoe, clearing the

A marvellous photograph of ploughing teams.

ground between three rows at a time) - one man leading the horse, the other guiding the machine. This was still rather slow but much easier and faster than hand hoeing. It used to take in the region of 10 days to complete hoeing. By that time, near the end of May, shearing of the sheep would commence. A man could catch his sheep and tie the fleeces at somewhere at the speed of 8 or 9 an hour. So, 300 ewes and possibly 180 lambs took several days to complete. The clippers were now driven by a small petrol engine. The first time I can remember shearing they were powered by a man, turning a huge cogged wheel with a chain attached to a very small wheel. This drove the clippers, thus enabling the man turning to keep a steady pace. What a tedious job!

Another boring job in May was weeding the corn fields of thistles, docks and charlock. This was done by using a pole about the size of a broomstick with a chisel-shaped tool attached to it's end. The creeping thistle was the worst weed, and some fields were covered with thousands and thousands of these weeds. We had to chop them off below ground-level, one at a time with the weeding iron on a stick. The idea being that although this would not kill the thistle, it would retard their growth allowing the corn to grow and help to smother further growth. If not done, the corn would be infested with thistles, thus making it very prickly to handle in making stacks in the field, making ricks and threshing. So, it was essential to do the job well or pay later on.

We were coming to the beginning of June and in the first week, weather permitting, we would start the hay harvest. George, the horse-man, would get up at day-break and before the sun became too hot and would cut some 3 acres of grass. If not too hot, would cut another 2 acres by mid-day. We found that 5 acres was enough to handle at any one time and no more would be cut until those 5 acres were nearly ready to cart into the Dutch barns in the yard. When the process would start over again - cutting, turning, tedding to dry crop and then carting to the barn.

If the weather was really hot and dry, some four days was required but, if cloudy and not very hot perhaps up to 8 days. So, when making hay you were in the lap of the Gods regarding the weather you needed. The same procedure as carting the corn was followed: 2 or perhaps 3 men in the field - 1 or 2 loading, one load making a tricky job on our steep meadows, 1 man taking carts from the field and yard and visa-versa. Two or three men in the yard pitching hay off carts and rick-making. Two or four acres could be cleared in a short day - 2.30pm to 8.30pm

If the hay was nearly fit (dry) to take to the Dutch barn and rain looked imminent, it would be poked in the field - a horse-drawn rake was used to put hay in rows across the field. Then came the rest of the staff armed with picks (two-pronged forks) and put the hay in heaps (pokes). These were cone-shaped, always kept high in the middle to keep or drain off any rain. The next day, if dry, was spread over the ground to dry and then carted to the yard. If wet, it would stay in pokes for days until the weather cleared. Weed were cut in the month of July. Corn-field hedges were trimmed, mangels hoed for the second time and swedes, if grown, hoed and singled.

I hope this gives you some idea of the workings of a mixed farm. The various jobs. The seasons. The different types of stock. The cropping, harvesting, sheep dipping and shearing. You needed to be a Jack-of-all-trades and, if lucky, master of at least some. Hard but happy days. But a shadow was appearing, as Hitler started his annexing parts of Europe. Why had we not taken the warnings given by Winston Churchill for many years prior? What a mistake.

❊

CHAPTER FIVE
A CLOUD ON THE HORIZON

In my second year on the farm, 1938-39, much the same pattern of work was carried out. The mood of the country changed as people realised that the possibility of war was getting more likely as the weeks went by. We were given some comfort when Neville Chamberlain came back from a meeting with Hitler, with a little piece of paper claiming 'Peace in our time'. A few weeks later the peace was shattered when Hitler invaded Poland and we were at war; a war that was to change so many lives and shatter so many dreams. It would last for nearly six long years, and great was the price paid by all involved.

Farmers were told what they had to grow. More corn, and large acreages of potatoes to help feed the nation. People at last realised what an important job farmers did, and how important they were to the war effort.

Nothing much happened in the first six months of the war then, in the spring of 1940 the German armoured divisions ran wild, avoiding the French Maginot Line by out-flanking defences and going through the Low Countries in a matter of a few days.

We were defeated all along the line, the German panzers had our troops were hemmed in against the sea at Dunkirk. Defeated and waiting to be rescued, were taken by sea in any seaworthy craft available, to England. What a disaster. Then, to cap it all, France capitulated and Hitler was in control of Western Europe. Very grave days indeed. Luckily for us, Hitler made the fatal error of thinking that we would give in and make peace on his terms. Or, failing that, he thought could bomb us into submission with his vast numbers of aircraft. Fortunately, the courage and skill of 'The Few' inflicted such losses, that he had to call off his daylight bombing raids. This was probably our greatest hour in the history of our nation, as stated by Winston Churchill.

Hitler then turned his armed might on Russia. At first it seemed that he could have been right, as he swept ever deeper into Russian territory. But, as his lines of communication became longer, his advance became slower and winter arrived with Moscow, Leningrad and Stalingrad still firmly in Russian hands. Perhaps the winter weather, the snow and bitter cold, were the Russians' greatest ally. They were used to these conditions and had the right clothes to keep warm whereas the Germans, not suitably clothed, were ill-equipped to deal with the harsh climate.

There were two things that saved us. First, Hitler's decision to attack Russia and second, the right man was at last given control of our country, Winston Churchill. A real bulldog, a great fighter and a blunt and truthful leader. It was as though history had given us the right man at the right time. A man we felt we could trust, a man we felt that despite all that had happened could eventually lead us to victory. We knew that this would or could not be done overnight, so we prepared ourselves for a long and hard struggle.

I remember certain phrases used by Churchill in his wartime speeches: 'Never in the field of human conflict have so many owed so much to so few'; 'All I can offer you is sweat, toil and blood'; 'When they come to write the history of this war and this country they will say, "This was their finest hour".'; 'We shall fight on the beaches, we will never give in". He gave us confidence, hope, the will to fight on and the courage to withstand the terrible battering our cities received from the air. The apalling casualties and devastation made us more determined than ever to see it through. Yes, they were dark days indeed.

I think the mood and determination of the country was shown when the Local Defence Volunteers (L.D.V.) later known as the Home Guard (H.G.) were formed. It was just after Dunkirk when we expected the Germans to invade. Although desperately short of weapons (all our heavy equiment was left at Dunkirk) we were determined to defend our land with whatever weapons we could find. I forget how we were told of the first meeting of the L.D.V. (H.G.) but we found ourselves on a bit of waste ground at the bottom of Codden Hill, with anything that would make some sort of weapon. I shall never forget the weapons on show; hooks, long-handled forks, air guns, and poles with knives attached to their ends. I had a shot-gun and six cartridges, so was easily the best armed of the lot. What good we would have been against the Germans, had they come, doesn't bear thinking of. It did show the determination, the will and the spirit that swept through the country at that time. That, I am sure, eventually won the war.

I remember my days in the L.D.V. (H.G.). The fun we had and the training we did. Most able-bodied men not doing military service were in the L.D.V. We did a lot of drill which, in my opinion, was rather a waste of time as many members of the L.D.V. were 65 to 70 years old. After a few weeks our platoon was issued with a few Lee Enfield rifles, so we learned to slope arms, etc. At some time later, about 8 to 12 months, we were issued with Home Guard (as we were now labelled) uniforms: leggings, boots and caps. We now looked a bit more like soldiers. We were still very short of rifles but we did get a little practice on the rifle range, a step in the right direction at last. We were sent one night to guard the railway station at Barnstaple, eight of us in all. Six in the waiting room, bedding down or making tea, two on patrol armed with .303 rifles. We were told that if we met anyone we were to challenge, asking if 'friend or foe'. We saw no one. Perhaps it was just as well, as we had to keep the one round of ammunition we had in our pocket and if the answer had been 'foe', we should have had to take the round from the pocket, open the breech of the rifle and load! I suppose the 'foe' was supposed to stand still while all this was going on. What a hope!

Some time in 1941 I was asked if I would like to join a secret and special branch of the H.G., an underground movement with secret bases in woods, old mines and quarries in North Devon. There were four of these underground units set up in North Devon. One in the Torrington Area, another in the Braunton Area, another at Snapper and ours, deep in Tawstock Woods. Although we often all trained together, we were not allowed to visit other bases. The thought being, that if captured we could not give away the other secret hideouts. The job was very interesting. We were given special treatment and each had a special pass which enabled us to travel anywhere, and could not be questioned on reasons or why we were there, or what we were doing. We were well armed, with one Browning gun, 8 sten guns, 8 Colt revolvers and a wicked dagger. We also did a bit of unarmed combat. We were taught the ways to use explosives and became experts in setting booby-traps and blowing things up.

Each unit consisted of 8 men, the oldest being 68 years of age the youngest 19. Our leader was a retired bank manager, a farmer's son. He had vast knowledge of the counryside and its ways - a very fit man for his age, 68 years. He was a man you could trust and have confidence in his leadership.

The next senior by age was a farmer, rather plump with a bald head. He would have made a good Humpty-Dumpty. Again, reasonably agile, was a crack shot and a good chap to have if you were in a tight corner.

Then came his brother, an expert in explosives. He had been an engineer with Leyland trucks. Where he got his knowledge of explosives from, I never found out but he definitely knew the tricks of the trade, which we all benefited from.

Two brothers were next senior, both had worked on the Tawstock Court estate since leaving school, as gamekeeper, underkeeper and gardener. They were both rather on the thin side - very active and tough with, vast knowledge of the woods, and they were able to make themselves disappear with the stealth they used in dealing with poachers. They were both able to look after themselves and could be a rough handful if needs be when aroused. Both were crack shots - a great asset to our unit. I suppose they were about forty years old. One was now a farmer, the other a full time gardener.

Perhaps the weakest link in the chain was the next member in rank. He, too, was a full time gardener. He was slightly lame, the result of a bad accident some years back. I don't think he would have been a great asset in time of crisis. Perhaps I am wrong and he would have done really well, but he was the only member that I had no confidence in.

Next came me. Rash, according to our leader. I saw no fear and was fit with tons of stamina. I could improvise very well and, like the others, determined to do my bit to make it unpleasant for 'Jerry', if he came.

I enjoyed the training in explosives, booby-traps and the mock attacks we did on military bases: R.A.F. Chivenor, a gun emplacement at Instow, radar station at Hartland, Railway Stations, the H.Q. at Fremington House and block houses at Northam Burrows.

Last, but not least, a pal of mine, a farmer's son from the farm next to ours. Tough and reliable perhaps like me, rash, and saw no or little fear and was very fit. Although he joined much later, he soon picked up the basics of the explosives, which would have been our main task if we had been invaded.

All the eight members of our unit had vast knowledge of the countryside and could have lived and managed, without too much trouble, in our bases and hide-outs for many weeks.

At our main base in Tawstock Woods, we had 1 cwt. of high explosives, Mills bombs, plenty of ammunition for weapons, enough food for at least a month and many cans of water. As the base was in the woods, the earth was always covered in dead leaves. These were glued to our trap-door which let us down to our base, and was well-nigh impossible to see with the carpet of leaves which covered the wood's floor. We also had three other secret hide-holes in the area, where one could hide but had few supplies.

During our training, we had to attack many military bases in North Devon. The first was the R.A.F. Station at Chivenor. We made a real mess of that base. They had guarded the base well around the land side but had left the river side wide open. We rowed or drifted on to it with a couple of boats from Instow, a mile or so downstream, and landed with no trouble. We left every aircraft marked with a swastika, in chalk, on their bodies. We came in and went back undetected (by this time the tide had turned). A job well done.

Another time we attacked the gun emplacement at Instow. Although we suffered many casualties, I managed to slip in to a line of prisoners, unnoticed, and when taken into the base let off my large 'thunder flash' (which could have been a grenade or small bomb). I should have perished with the rest but the gun emplacement would have been blown up, and all of us with it.

Another time we attacked rolling stock at Barnstaple station. Although they had been warned of attack, we again did terrible damage with our make-believe chalk swastikas. All the engines and much of the rolling stock would have been immobilized. We suffered only light casualties.

If the Germans had come, we would have done quite a bit of damage to trains, booby-trapped the roads and bridges, and transport in general. How long we would have lasted, I do not know, but we were told to always carry our phial of poison containing Potassium and if captured, or if village people were held hostage, we would have the choice then of them or me? Thank God this was never put to the test.

Our main Base, in Tawstock Woods, was shaped like half a ball. The straight side was the front of the Base, a small hollow or quarry, the front built up with earth, bushes, dead pieces of trees. This sloped to match the bank on either side. A large amount of moss was also used. Inside, there was a seat around the circular side, with 3ft. boards nailed to the framework around the back and above and behind the bench or seat.

One panel of boards could be removed, behind which was our escape tunnel about 3ft. wide and 4ft. high and running some 25yds. to another hollow in the ground at the end of another trap door. This could only be opened from inside, the outside being covered with moss and dead brushwood and nearly impossible to see from the outside.

The base itself was booby-trapped with triggering wires in the safety chamber (see drawing overleaf). What we hoped would be our safety chamber, had two doors which could be closed, allowing the main blast of the booby-trap to go straight down the escape tunnel. The two doors, one in the main base and one in the safety chamber, would help protect us from the blast. There were six booby-traps outside, just below ground, which could all be set off at the push of a button. We were as well protected as possible. Anyone within 30yds. of the Base, on the outside, would have been lucky if not killed.

Would our protection from the blast inside have worked? We shall never know. When the war ended, we had some almighty bangs as we were ordered to destoy our store of explosives.

I think the country and its people should feel ashamed at the way we thanked Churchill for his

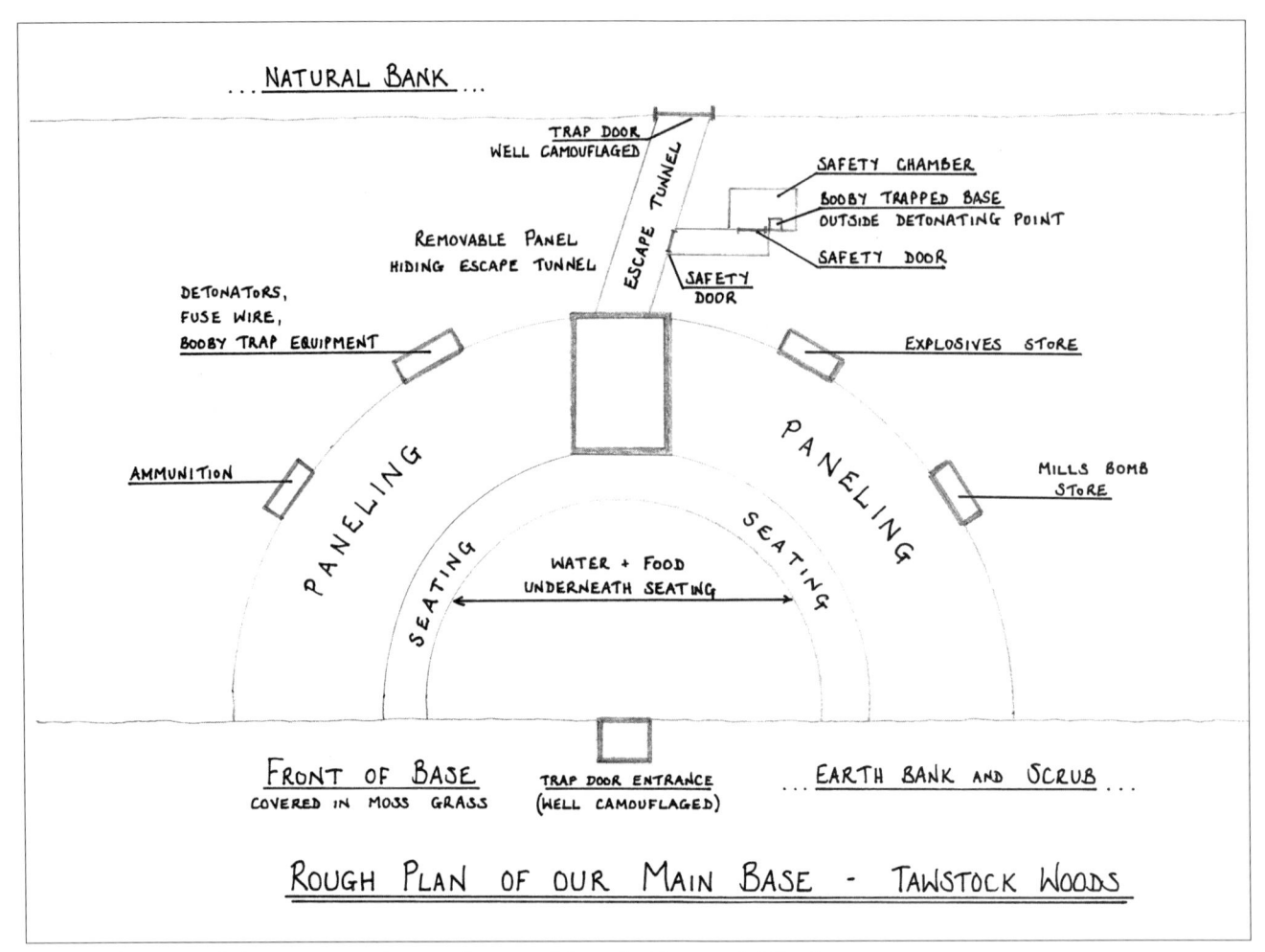

A plan drawing of the secret wartime underground base in Tawstock Woods.

great leadership. We had an election and threw him out of office. What he must have felt, I dread to think. What thanks. I was proud of my country, proud to be an Englishman but ashamed at the way we had treated the greatest leader this country has ever had.

CALL UP PAPERS

In the summer of 1940, my brother and I both decided to volunteer to join the R.A.F. We did not tell one another of this decision. It was only when our call-up papers arrived, telling us where to take our medical, that we knew of the other's intention.

Thus a fierce argument ensued, as we realised that one of us had to stay at home to help run the farm. He claimed that, being the eldest, he had the right to volunteer before me. That it was his duty as elder brother to protect me. I was having none of this, and told him so, claiming that if there had been no war I would probably have now been at a school of drama and music. Therefore, as farming was definitely his way of life, I should go before him. Neither of us would give way, although we accepted it was not right that we should leave Dad on his own, and that we were doing an important job in providing food for the nation.

What were we to do? We did agree that one should go and one should stay, but which one? As neither of us would give in, we decided to spin a coin. If it came down heads, he would go, if tails, I would go. The future lives of both of us would be decided by tossing up a coin. It came down heads up, he would go and I would stay. That was how our future was decided.

Dad had to apply to the Agricultural Board, saying he could not do without me on the farm, and stating that as mine was a reserved occupation, that I be released from my medical due in ten days, thus cancelling my application to join the R.A.F.

I knew then, that I should never do anything but farming as a career. I could not live with the thought that I had sheltered in farming during the war and when at last it would end, say 'thank you very much, I'm off on another career'.

The spinning of that coin had decided so much for me. I found it very frustrating being in a safe job, when my pals were facing great danger on land, air and sea. And when one was killed, I felt so bitter at having no chance to take my revenge.

WORK ON THE FARM - 1941-1945

The work on the farm was hard, and long hours were worked in producing as much food as possible, the only consolation being that at least I was helping in doing a very essential job. But it never made up for not being side by side with my pals out there.

Living on a farm had its blessings. In those days of food rations, we had all the cream and butter one could want. We were allowed to kill two pigs a year. We had poultry when needed and plenty of wild rabbit.

So, from the meat side, we were pretty well off but were the same as everyone else for tea, cheese, soap, currants, sultanas and sugar. Tins of fruit were few and far between, but the country folk or farmers had a great advantage over the town people at that time. Petrol was strictly rationed, so we had to plan the use of the car to make our meagre allowance first do the essential journeys and if any left over, perhaps the odd journey for pleasure.

About 1941, the Land Girls came into being. They were of great help at potato picking time, harvest and apple picking. A jolly hard working lot of girls.

After my brother went in the early summer of 1941, we were one short in the workforce on the farm, so we needed to find some time-saving tools to help us keep pace with the work. It was then that Dad ordered our first tractor, an Allis Chalmers B. Not very big, but a real workhorse wonder. I could plough four acres a day, compared with one acre by horses. The same applied in time-saving on most arable work. With haulage, we could take up to two tons compared with a half or three-quarters of a ton by horse. The same applied to cutting grass or corn - about three times the acreage per hour. So, with saving in time, we managed to carry on with one hand less.

My brother had passed his medical O.K. and was sent to America to train as a pilot, or member of the air crew. He would be there for the next six months.

Our system of farming had now greatly changed, to meet the demands of basic foods to feed the nation. Whereas we used to grow 20 to 25 acres of corn, we now grew 80 to 100 acres. Where before we grew no potatoes, we now grew 5 acres. This meant a reduction in numbers of sheep and cattle kept on the farm. If we could supply enough wheat and potatoes, at least the people would not starve. Perhaps a diet of bread and potatoes, though not very exciting, would help keep hunger at bay.

We had double summer-time at that time and were often working in the harvest field until 11.30pm or midnight. Very hard and tiring work. In the winter we had a little more time to spare, with less livestock to look after, and were able to take life a little easier. Now my brother was away, I had to find someone to help me keep the rabbits under control. There was an ex-farmer and keeper living in a thatched house just across the valley. A few years prior, he had ceased farming his 25 acres and Father had purchased the farm and house with condition that he and his wife could live in the house, rent free, for the rest of their lives.

Now, at the age of 75, he helped me with ferreting, tilling nets in holes on his side of the hedge and catching any rabbits trying to escape that way. I had nets and guns on my side and between us we managed to keep the rabbits under control. His wife was terribly lame, one leg being much shorter than the other, but when I called to see them (as I often did on cold winter days) they were snug and warm with a good fire going with their store of logs and coal. The kettle was always at hand and a cup of tea went down well. Their talk of years gone were of great interest. They never had much in life. They had both worked hard but had not had the best of luck. They never complained and were happy with what they had. They had one another - were a real 'Derby and Joan' - a really grand old couple.

He had a large garden and small orchard (apples and plums). The garden was very sheltered and warm with peaches and pears along one wall. Somehow he always managed to dig new potatoes, grown out of doors (no glass cloches) by his birthday, on 12 May - a remarkable feat. They were about the size of hen eggs. He was a master gardener.

At the end of 1940, the girls of the Land Army became available to help the farmers. They were, on the whole, hard-working and happy and a great help at busy times, such as harvest, threshing, apple picking and the potato harvest. In those days, potatoes were dug by machine but had to be picked up from the ground by hand, placed into buckets and emptied into bags which were later picked up, and loaded onto trailers then carted off to the store. These girls spent weeks or months on end in this back-breaking and hard job. They were a real asset to the war effort, and many farmers would have found great difficulty in getting work done without their aid.

My brother, after spending six months in America, moved on to Canada. He failed to become a pilot but became navigator and bomb aimer. It was now 1941. He was nearly ready, his training nearly over, he would soon be on raids to Germany or elsewhere.

Back on the farm, work went on in the usual way. Long hours, especially at harvest, but a bit less hectic on short winter days.

The farmhouse home of Mr and Mrs Parker, across the valley from Overton.

Mr and Mrs Parker.

WAR NEWS

The best news on the war front was that the German advance in Russia had been halted, and many German divisions were bogged down there. Some of the worst news of the war years were (perhaps not in the order of happening) at sea, the sinking of the battleship *Hood*, followed by the *Prince of Wales*. Then, either the *Renown* or *Repulse* by the Japanese. Three of our greatest ships. Then came the fall of Singapore and Malaisia to the Japs; the fall of Crete and Tobruk to the Germans, whose advance was stopped just short of Egypt. We lost a colossal amount of shipping sunk by packs of U-boats.

Despite all these set-backs, we felt we could still win the war. The Japs made the fatal mistake of bombing Pearl Harbor, sinking many ships of the U.S. Fleet. This awakened 'Uncle Sam', and America was now at war with Germany and Japan. At last we were not still alone with Russia and our Colonies but had the power of the U.S.A. on our side, in Europe and the far East.

The first bright spot was when the light cruiser, *Exeter* and destroyers *Ajax* and *Achilles*, took on the might of the pocket-battleship, the *Graf Spee*, and forced it to seek shelter up the river plate. Although only the badly damaged the British ships were waiting for her off the River Plate. She never again did battle, and scuttled herself at the mouth of the river; a great victory. Then the *Bismark*, the pride of the German Navy, (she had sunk the *Hood* and badly damaged *The Prince of Wales*) escaped into the Atlantic Ocean, where it could do terrific damage to our shipping lines. It had to be found and sunk at all costs. There were no British ships near enough to engage the *Bismark*. Our only hope were the 'Swordfish' torpedo bombers to find and cripple the German monster. These planes were slow and real death-traps. How many were lost, I do not know, but one managed to score a hit on the stern of the *Bismark*, damaging her steering. She could now only steam around in a large circle. This gave us time for the battleship *Duke of York* to get in range and also, with the aid of some destroyers and their torpedoes, managed to send the *Bismark* to the bottom of the sea. Revenge for the brave 'Swordfish' pilots and the crew of H.M.S. *Hood*.

Later on, with the aid of America, we defeated Rommel in Africa and Libya and the North African coast was now under our control. Next came Sicily then Italy, and after a bloody and long drawn-out battle, lasting many months, were now under allied control. Meanwhile, our bombers were giving the Germans some of their own medicine. Their towns and industrial areas were bombed incessantly, but a great cost.

BACK HOME

There was not a great deal going on in the entertainment world during the war. A few dances here and there. Quite a few concerts in villages to raise money for parcels for boys serving in the Forces. I used to sing in many of these, which brought back a pang of what it could have been. Young Farmers Clubs, with monthly meetings, was somewhere to go and usually quite interesting. Cinemas were open and were usually full. How we drove cars on dark nights, with masks on the head-lights throwing a beam on the road about 6ft. in front of the vehicle, I shall never know. Beer and spirits were often hard to come by, especially when the Yanks were here in thousands, training for the invasion of Europe still yet to come. We could now see the light at the end of the tunnel, with the

Russians starting to push the Germans back. The Japs had been stopped in their tracks. The war was slowly turning in our favour. Then came D-Day. Our forces landed in Normandy, and although suffering many casualties, had at last a bridge-head in Europe. Thus, with mounting pressure from the Russians in the East and the allies in the West with superior air power, this was the beginning of the end of this long drawn-out war. It dragged on until the following spring when the Germans, defeated on all fronts, surrendered and sought peace at last. Two atomic bombs dropped on the Japs, made them seek peace. A few months later peace reigned, in the place of war. Millions of lives had been lost and many millions more ruined. What a price we had paid to ensure that people would be free from tyranny and racial injustice, and be able to express their minds without fear. We had stood alone at the beginning, defying the greatest military power in the world.

We can be justly proud of the part we played and of the men who never returned.

CHAPTER SIX
HOME ON LEAVE

My brother came home on leave at the end of August, 1943, he had a three-day break. On the Friday, being market day and nothing hurting on the farm, we decided to go to town. We chatted to many friends, among them was a girl call May, a farmer's daughter, whom I had known casually for a number of years. My brother asked her if she would like to join us for a drink that evening. She said, 'yes'.

I had someone in tow, so was quite happy to make a foursome. Somehow an old flame of my brother's turned up and we were five. May was very quick-tempered, and soon made an excuse to leave. As he had really finished with his old flame none of us stayed long, and a good evening was spoilt. On the Sunday, I took my friend to Instow, some eight miles distant on the Torridge estuary, quite a pleasant little village. My brother said he would like to call and see May and apologise for the mix-up. As it was on the way to Instow, I agreed to take him along. He apologised and she agreed to come to Instow with us.

We dropped her off on the way home, and I remember him saying that perhaps they could meet on his next leave. The next day he returned to his base. He told me that he had two more flights to do, then he would have done thirty and would be rested for some time. The aircraft he flew in was a Sterling, which was probably the worst of our bombers as it had a ceiling of about 18,000ft. and therefore an ideal target for the German anti-aricraft batteries. He had a shrapnel wound in his shoulder, to prove the point, on his last leave. A week went by, perhaps he had completed his thirty flights and would have earned a well-deserved rest, with the other members of the crew.

On the Saturday I was ferreting, with my old keeper friend, in a field just behind the farmhouse, when the herdsman came running across the field towards us. He said I was wanted by the rest of the family, as my brother was reported missing, shot down on a raid over Germany. I was stunned. It could not happen on his last flight, or next to last flight. Surely fate could not be that unkind. With my mind in a whirl, I made my way to the house and family. They, too, were numb and stunned by the telegram. Father said nothing and went upstairs to his bedroom, and was missing for the next half an hour. I pointed out that even though he was missing, he could still be alive, we did not know for certain that he was dead. We had been through many scrapes together, I was sure he would somehow get out of this one. This was the slight hope to which we would cling. In a matter of days, the worst news came confirming he had been killed. If the coin had come down tails, perhaps it would have been me. I felt all the bitterness again, at being tied at home on the farm

Lest we forget... HRH Queen Elizabeth (now the Queen Mother), greets newly trained RAF recruits, among them the author's brother (standing centre looking at the camera).

with no chance of getting my revenge. No outlet for my feelings, just sheer frustration. Perhaps some of those feelings are portrayed in some of the poems I wrote at that time. Perhaps they were my safety-valve. I don't know, but I suddenly realised that my parent's hopes and dreams rested on my shoulders to fulfill. Also, that my sister would only have me to help look after her when my parents had gone - a very sobering point. This was probably the lowest point in my life. We were very close as brothers, done so many things together. He had been my idol, now he was gone like so many others. He could never be replaced, and the fact that he had gone instead of me, did not help.

Dad had a younger brother who farmed the old family farm near Bishops Nympton. He and his kind family, sensing that Christmas would be a sad time for us, insisted that we spent some time with them. This helped greatly in raising my spirits.

When my brother was reported missing, I wrote May a note, as I had heard him say he would hope to meet her on his next leave. I thought she should be told of the sad news. She replied, suggesting that we should meet and talk as we had known one another for some time. I thought it quite a good idea. Any rate, I needed someone to cheer me up and she was full of life and fun, it would probably do me the world of good. So, a few days later, we met. I think we drove somewhere and sat talking in the car. Although we had occasionally danced together, we had never really talked and knew very little about each other. I think we both knew we were a pair of flirts and both had little trouble in dating our opposite sex. We found out that we were both musical, May playing and singing and me just singing. Both knew many ballads of that time and both of us had sung quite a few as solos. We both had a love of the country, liked the same type of films, were both from farming stock, so, had a great deal in common. We agreed that we had enjoyed each other's company and should meet again. There being a decent film on, the following week, we decided to go and see it. That's how it all started. Little did we know, at that time, it was the end of our flirting days. Here we are today, 52 years on!

CHAPTER SEVEN
OUR WEDDING DAY

We were engaged on May's birthday, and married on mine, 5 September, 1945. The war was ended but things were far from normal.

We held the reception on the lawn, in a marquee at May's home. It was a sit-down affair: plates of cold meat, salad potatoes, rolls and butter, trifles, fresh fruits, various pies, cheese, wine, champagne, coffee and tea. Where all the food came from was a miracle, as food was strictly rationed in those days. A bit of fiddling must have gone on somewhere.

For our honeymoon, we were first going for a few nights to Blackpool and then on to Scotland. Remember, there were no cars produced during the war so we had an eight-year-old Austin 10. If you accelerated in full downhill, you may have obtained a speed of 50m.p.h. The roar of the engine was such, that conversation was impossible. As petrol was strictly rationed, we cadged from all our friends and with a car tank full and 30 gallons in containers in the boot, and with a few coupons in reserve, we set off. The day before the wedding, I took the car to the pub at East Anstey adjoining the railway line, so when we left for our honeymoon we had to take a taxi to Barnstaple and then catch a train to East Anstey. This all went quite smoothly, and the crackers under the train wheels gave us a good send-off. When we arrived at East Anstey the landlady, guessing that we were just married, had invited her locals to wish us well. So we had a fair session before setting out for Taunton, where we were spending our first night. On arriving at Taunton we were greeted by an elderly porter, and when we had signed the register, he told me that, as someone had told him that I was suffering from a chill, he had put hot water-bottles in the bed as asked to do. I don't think we really needed hot water-bottles that night! The next morning, after breakfast, we took our cases to the car to find we had two flat tyres. What a start! We had to get a garage to come and mend the punctures. Remember, tyres were very hard to come by in the war years and if you had a set with no gaiters or canvas showing, you were very well shod. About 10.30am we set off for Blackpool. Not an easy journey No sign-posts, no town names and no motorways. I had never been further than Gloucester, so just had to hope for the best. We did pretty well until we came to Preston, when we came back to the same roundabout three times. Someone who was watching, stopped us on the third time saying, 'E lad, I think thou be lost!' and asked where were we going? I told him, and he told us where to go and finally we arrived at our destination at 10.00pm. What a journey! We saw the sights of Blackpool from its tower, but not the lights. They had not been switched on since the

Our wedding day.

war. We were there for three days, then moved on to Dumfries in Scotland. The only thing I remember about the hotel, was trying to eat porridge without sugar - horrid. I tried salt - more horrid. We managed to get as far north as Edinburgh, a very beautiful city. We dared not try to go too far, or we could run out of petrol. We enjoyed what we saw of Scotland, and have been back twice and enjoyed both times. One was a fishing trip and the other was sight-seeing and touring. We broke the journey home at Liverpool, staying a night with friends. We arrived home on the Sunday, and just to break us in had two days threshing on Monday and Tuesday!

CHAPTER EIGHT
NOW TO WORK

My parents and sister moved to their new home in Barnstaple on the Thursday, so we were alone in a huge house that had been so full of people in my boyhood days. We decided to let two rooms downstairs and two bedrooms upstairs. We would give them the use of the bathroom three days a week. They had their own toilet for the sum of 25 shillings per week, which went a long way towards the housekeeping. New furniture was all utility and had to be purchased with 'furniture dockets'. The curtains were on 'coupons', as were blankets, linen, tablecloths, etc. They soon ate up our meagre ration of dockets or coupons. Mum left behind a large settee, a huge side-board, dining-table, oak-top desk and a few odd chairs and benches. So, by buying half a dozen chairs and a kitchen table, a few rugs and a secondhand carpet (all utility), we made do. We managed to get a couple of second-hand armchairs. We did not know, but there would be no decent new furniture for at least two years. We kept the open hearth fire burning during the winter, for warmth and for keeping the huge kettle on the boil - it also made lovely toast. We had a lad living-in who, like me, had a healthy appetite so we kept May busy cooking, a job she soon became quite good at.

Our farming outside was very like the last years of the war. Most things were still strictly rationed and would be for another two to two and a half years. Things in general were very slowly getting back to normal. One thing that had gone was the 'blackout'. After nearly six years, it was great to see the lights at night once again, both in the street and from the house windows. Where all had been black and sullen, were now bright and shining, giving new hope. When driving a car without the headlight masks, what a relief to at last be able to see where you were going. Although petrol was still rationed we could, with good management, use the car locally sometimes for pleasure. The worst was over, we at last had peace, the scars still remained and a huge job lay ahead to rebuild our cities laid to waste in 1940. Many thousands of men and women would be swapping their uniforms for civilian clothes and would now require civilian jobs and settle down to a quieter way of life. What a huge upheaval there was bound to be.

I was lucky to have a farm. Although not owning it, I had it at a pretty low rent. I had a job and a living, perhaps not the one I would have chosen under different circumstances, but now my way of life. I was my own boss. Whether we made a success or failure was up to May and me, as a farmer's wife still played a part, and in many ways was a partner, with her seeing to the poultry, cream, apples and garden produce side of things.

Poultry on the farm: Top left: May in the rearing house.

Above: Our flock of geese (How many shopping days to Christmas?).

Left: May with the hen flock.

We had both come from farming, so knew what was needed and what would have to be done. It was on this basis we started our married life and a farming career.

I don't think anything outstanding happened on the farm at that time. We had a ready market for our produce: meat, potatoes, wheat, barley, milk, eggs and apples. These were still badly needed to feed the nation and were on guaranteed prices, fixed by the government, so at least we knew the price we would get for the finished article. Also, that there would be a market for it.

The Women's Land Army was disbanded about that time, although many of the girls married country folk and many still worked on the farms. They preferred their country life, its slow rhythm to the mad rush and overcrowding in our busy cities.

About 1946 we did increase the poultry side on our farm. Keeping about 200 hens free-range and fattening turkeys and geese for the Christmas trade. Also, Indian game crosses for chicken at Christmas. This meant that the farm kitchen came into use once again. I used to stun, kill and bleed the birds, pull out large wing and tail feathers outside on a line, and then bring them into the kitchen where three or four people would finish the plucking. May and another lady would do the 'drawing' (removing the innards) from the birds, dressing them off with liver, hearts, gizzards and fat from the insides of the birds. They then had the job of weighing, and then labelling with people's names who had ordered for their Christmas dinners. They were a real treat to look at, lined up on the slate slabs in the old dairy to set and keep cool. The food on plucking days was usually cups of tea and sandwiches and other cold snacks. There were too many feathers flying around to have a sit-down meal, and the old kitchen table was being used for drawing and dressing of birds. I suppose a chicken took 15 to 20 minutes, a turkey 20 minutes and a goose up to half or three-quarters of an hour, to pluck. So, depending on the number of birds and the number of pluckers, it took either one or two days. They were happy days in the warmth of the kitchen. Plenty of chatter and, although tiring work, enjoyed by all. A turkey would weigh 10 to 20lbs., the price 25 shillings a pound. The geese 10 to 14lbs. and 27 shillings and 6 pence per pound. A chicken 6 to 8lbs. at £1 per pound. This was always regarded as the farmer's wife's perks, to help buy a Christmas present and the goodies for Christmas. We must have turned our good tasting and tender birds because the same people had them year after year.

CHAPTER NINE
CHRISTMAS TIME AND RABBITING PARTIES

On Christmas Day, half the staff did just the jobs that had to be done, such as feeding the stock, milking for household use and mucking out. The other half did the same on Boxing Day, so at least you had one day off for the Christmas period.

On Christmas Day, my parents and sister spent the day with May and me, and on Boxing Day May and I joined her family at her brother, Arthur's, who was farming the farm where May was born. We were joined by May's two other brothers and her sister, together with her father and mother. So, altogether, a large gathering compared with my small family on Christmas day.

We had a lot of rabbiting and card parties at this time of the year. The men used to go early in the morning, armed with ferrets and guns. They usually went into the house for coffee, when arriving at their destination. Lunch was usually carried, and a short stay in operations would take place about 1pm. This was quite good fun, with a bag of some twenty-five rabbits per pair (you always went in two's to cover each side of the Devon hedges.) The day usually ended about half-an-hour before dark.

The best day I ever had was with May's brother. We bagged 49, and only missed one all day but we could not find one more to make it 50. When we had finished ferreting we set out for home to wash,

May's family home at Litchardon.

put on a decent set of clothes, pick up our wives and arrive back in time for dinner, about 7.00pm. This was followed by cards until the early hours of the morning. Nap, pontoon, farmer's glory and brag were the most popular games, and perhaps at the end of the season you may have been £10 'in' or £10 'out'. If you were out, you had a lot of fun for your money. Perhaps it was just as well there were no breathylisers, as I am sure that on many occasions we would not have passed. But, despite

May's parents.

With May's Mum and Dad at Home.

A Meet outside May's family home at Litchardon

this, I cannot remember any accidents of any kind, we always arrived home safe and sound. The only other pleasures we had were the odd dance, a few Hunt Balls, the two local cinemas and our radios. In other words, you had to make a lot of your own entertainment.

A LITTLE POLICE WORK

In the Spring, Summer and early Autumn we were pretty busy on the farm, with only a few days off. When we did manage a short break, we went sightseeing and visiting local beaches. We had little time for anything else. Perhaps it is worth mentioning that I was persuaded to become a Special Constable, to help the local police. I attended many sessions of instruction and learnt a lot about the law, and what I could and could not do. I did very little 'beat' work but I remember standing to attention and saluting the Queen, when she passed through our village of Bishops Tawton in a Royal car on route to Exeter. When I retired, some years later, I was given a long-service medal. Never was a medal less deserved, I had done nothing to earn it.

CHAPTER TEN
WE'RE GOING TO BE PARENTS

In 1946 May and I were delighted when we realised she was pregnant, and that sometime in April or May we would be a proud Mum and Dad!

I know it was a hard winter, quite a bit of snow. May had a lot of day-old chicks to rear and that was a job she was expert at. She insisted on walking to the farm-rearing house in often very treacherous conditions under foot. I was not very happy, and was worried in case she slipped and hurt herself and the child she was carrying. She made a great job of rearing the chicks and came to no harm.

The winter seemed to fly by, and spring was upon us. Not long now - would it be a girl or boy? According to the doctor's forecast, sometime in early May - perhaps on May's birthday on the 10th. Sometime during the night on 9 April, May woke and said she had pains. I thought she must be mistaken, but realising that this was not the case rang the nursing home where she was booked to have the baby. I grabbed her case, already packed, and helped her down the stairs. I fetched the car and brought it to the door, helped her in, threw the case on the back seat and then off to the nursing home some 3 miles distant, at Barnstaple. I saw her settled and was told by the matron that I could do no good staying there, she would ring me if needed and let me know immediately when the baby was born. So, with some misgivings, I went home. I could not sleep as I was too worried and excited. I think I may have dozed off a few times. The telephone rang about 7 o'clock with the news we had a baby boy, 9lbs in weight just born, and I could come as soon as I liked - all was well. What a relief. What great joy that we had a son.

I did not take long to get dressed, had a quick cup of tea and then off. May was radiant holding her new born - she looked so proud. The baby had so much jet black hair that it was neatly parted, he really looked quite pretty. The doctor had been a bit out forecasting the month of May. It did not matter, we had a healthy nine pound son.

I spent the rest of the day telling my family and May's family the news and did not see May again until the evening. After a week, May and baby were allowed home. We were together again, and although things had somewhat changed with the new baby, we soon got used to it and life settled down once again, with a slightly different routine.

GETTING READY FOR THE CHRISTENING

The people living in part of our house were moving out, so we had rooms on our hands. We did not wish to let again, so had to start thinking about furnishing. There was still no furniture available in Barnstaple, except utility. We thought it would be nice if we could partly furnish one

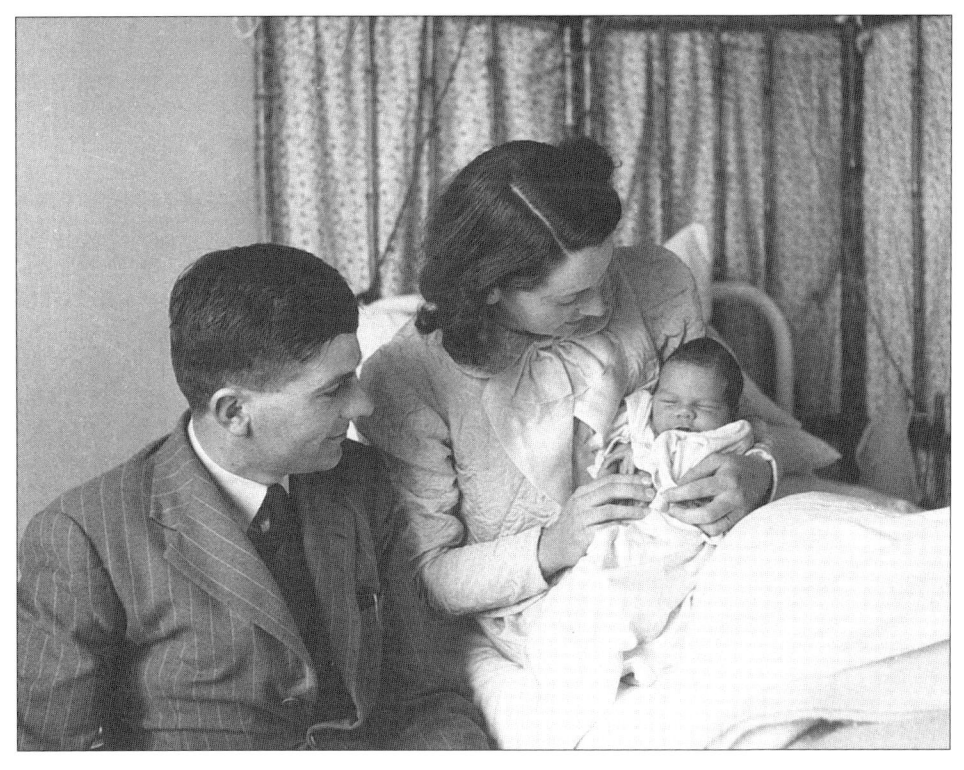

May and myself with John, just 24 hours old

room for the Christening of our son. We did see in one of the papers, a three-piece suite from a firm called Otezmen. We took a gamble and ordered one at a cost of £27.00. It arrived just in time, on the Saturday before the Sunday christening. With a second-hand carpet, a mirror over the fireplace, a small display cabinet, and a piano Mother had given us for our wedding present, the room did not look too bad. Although still scantily furnished, at least we were slowly getting there.

We had spent quite a bit of time, during the last two years, on the large lawn and flower garden which had been somewhat neglected during the war years. We had removed the pampas grass, the old monkey puzzle tree which only had a few of the top branches alive, and the old Yew tree. We ploughed and reseeded the lawn and made two rose borders, one rockery along the bank which ran full length of the lawn (some 25 yds.), and made a shrubbery at the west end to give shelter from the western gales. We broke up the lawn by taking out two flower beds. In fact, we had completely altered the layout and set out a new garden.

May was the designer, I helped with the hard work and enjoyed doing so. Between us we did a very good job. We did not realise how beautiful it would one day become.

The christening went off quite well. We were proud to show them our new suite, and said how lucky we were to have taken a chance and how nice it was.

When John was two years old, he gave us a real fright when he would not stop crying and kicking in pain. We discovered he had a large lump bulging out from his lower tummy. Thinking it might be something serious we rushed him to hospital, to find that he had a strangulated hernia. If we had not taken him in when we did, it could have burst, with dire results. Anyhow, we had caught it in time. He was operated on immediately and after about ten days, allowed home.

By this time, we had hoped John would have had a brother or sister but, sadly, this was not to be.

CODDEN HILL

Food was still scarce and we were encouraged to clean up any rough land and produce crops on it. Codden Hill, some 200 acres, was owned by three different farmers. They agreed to plough some 100 acres on the south side but leave the rest as it was growing bracken, gorse and heather. This caused ill feeling from the village of Bishops Tawton and many meetings were called, to enable a formula to be hammered out which would be acceptable to all concerned. We gave them permission to walk over all the Hill when out to grass. They promised to respect our crops, when ploughed, and also our wire fences. This agreement is still going on after forty-five years and is working well on both sides.

Peace and tranquility. The author stands on Codden Hill.

CHAPTER ELEVEN
SOME OF MY PUBLIC LIFE

In the early Fifties, I served on many agricultural connected committees. Devon County Show, Barnstaple Fatstock Show, The National Farmers Union, and the Parish Council. I later became Chairman of the Barnstaple N.F.U., President of the F.S. Show and judged Devon Cattle at many of the leading shows. I won a number of prizes with pig and lamb carcases, roots and hay. Though nothing compared with my Grandfather Huxtable.

Life was going pretty well in 1952. John was about to go to a small prep. school at Heanton, some six miles away, where he was to stay until he was nine. Then he went to a prep. school at Okehampton. Both these schools had the same name, 'Upcott House'. He did well at both schools, and was usually in the top four. He passed his entrance exam. for Blundels and at the age of twelve, spent the next four years there. He, like me, was not brilliant at sport but turned out to be an excellent cross-country runner. He finished school with many passes. There was no doubt what he wanted to be. He was going to be a farmer.

THE COMMITTEE and CHAIRMANSHIP N.F.U.

I think I should tell you of some of my memories, of things that happened on various committees I served on to do with farming, and my term of office as Chaiman of Barnstaple N.F.U.

During my Chairmanship of the N.F.U., nothing particular was achieved in the farming world but, nevertheless, I found the work very interesting. I used to go to Exeter, monthly, for county meetings, representing my branch. Like most councils, a lot of talk went on, resolutions were passed which we thought would benefit farmers. These were then forwarded to Central Office, sometimes debated and acted upon, but more often than not, left to gather dust.

We used to have a 'Plough Sunday' in February, at Braunton Parish Church, where the plough was blessed and I, being Chairman of the N.F.U., read the lesson. Whether this blessing did any good, I don't know, but at any rate it did no harm. We used to have an annual dinner at Bromleys Cafe, Barnstaple, when about 160 members would be present. There were a great number of toasts and speeches by leading members of many different bodies. Some good and some not so good after-dinner speakers. Anyhow, it was often 11.00pm or 11.30pm by the time they all had their say - rather unfair to the last speakers.

Also, on the lighter side, we had an annual cricket match against the auctioneers and dealers, held at Instow cricket ground. A beautiful ground, right against the sea, with views of Barnstaple bar and the Atlantic beyond - an ideal setting. There was a lovely old, thatched pavilion, with changing rooms and large dining room, together with bar

The author (right), with a fellow judge, W.Cole, at the Devon Cattle Breeder's Society annual show, Exeter, 1950.

and kitchen at the back. Being thatched it was always cool, even on the hottest days.

As Chairman of the N.F.U., one had to captain and pick the farmer's team no matter how good, or bad, your form at cricket. The game, although played in a fiendly atmosphere, was very keenly contested - pride was at stake. Both sides had some excellent cricketers; the game was not just hit or miss! Usually about 400 to 450 runs were scored. Sometimes we won, sometimes they did. Anyhow,

Annual farmers v. auctioneers cricket match at Instow, 1960. Back row l-r: S. Symons, H. Smale, J.Tucker, R. Budge, H. Balman, A. Bussel, M. Copp, A. Goar, D. Elworthy. Middle Row: J. Isaac (umpire); G. Stanbury, M. May, R. Balman, H. Bird, H. May, R. Smith, B. Stanbury, C. Price, G. Blackman (umpire). Front row: Scorer; J. Symons; F. Thorne; B. Verney, W. Sanders, (?) R. Wonnacott, T. Stanley.

the spectators were treated to some fine cricket.

I remember the year I was Captain. The weather was rather overcast and heavy, the swing bowlers had a good day and the match was over by about 4.00pm. We all adjourned to the bar (rather early to start drinking) so we had tea first and then the fun began. At about 7.00pm we decided we would have one for the road and then off home. We could not decide who should buy the last round, them or us? To settle this we, the captains, went outside and put two stumps in the ground. I would bat and he would bowl four balls. If the stumps were left intact, he would buy the beer - if shattered, then it would be me.

I knew that, at this time of day, I would have a job to see the ball clearly, and hoped that the same would apply to him when bowling. The first ball was a wide, the second I managed to get a thick edge, the third went over the top of the stumps and the fourth, I never saw. I paid for the beer. Thus ended a great day.

I served on many show committees, i.e. Devon

County, Instow (later North Devon), Fatstock and Dairy Shows. These two later combined, and became the North Devon Autumn Show.

Devon County took quite a bit of time. A day before the show took place (to make sure everything for your duties on the show days were complete and in order) and three days on show week (helping in any way needed). So, for show week, very little was done by the farmer at home.

The other shows were one-day events but stalls, pens, etc. had to be erected; parade rings fenced off; stewarding to be done on show days and clearing up to be carried out the day after the show. So, again, at least three days had to be set aside.

The Fatstock Show, near the end, was wrongly named. When I was first on the committee, mid to late forties, the fatter the animal the more chance of winning. But, in the early fifties, the words 'over fat' came into being and although the animal had to be well covered, 'very fat' became a minus, whereas it had always been a plus in bygone years.

During the fifties 'carcass classes' grew in popularity, as people wished to see what kind of meat they were eating. These classes were dominated by the meat companies, i.e. North Devon Meat, F.M.C., W.R. Yeo (dealer and slaughterer). They swept the board, thus taking nearly all the prizes. Not surprising, when you realise they all had hundreds of carcasses to pick from. The real farmer had no chance. To help redress this, I suggested that all animals to be shown should be ear-tagged, alive, on the Monday at their places of slaughter. When slaughtered, the head was to be left on until inspected by a member of the Committee, who would read the ear-tag, then stamp the carcass with a special stamp and show number. Thus, although the meat companies and dealers would still have many more live animals to pick from, they would not have the advantage of seeing them all hung up as carcasses, before doing so. I, being the instigator of this scheme, was given the job with another committee member, of carrying out the tagging and stamping of the animals - a short two days work.

I am glad to say that this broke the monopoly of the meat companies and dealers; farmers now appeared in the prize lists. The skill of carcass showing, is being able to pick the right animal when alive, and being able to foresee what it will be like when dead.

These shows are no longer there, as they were. The Instow Show has now become the North Devon Show and is now held at Landkey - thriving and healthy. The Fatstock Show was a great sight in years long gone. One of the high-lights of the farming year, Barnstaple Fatstock Show, was known as the 'Smithfield of the South West'. In the thirties it was well supported by most people in the farming world, and many people from our towns. It was a must and a social occasion. I remember the beautiful layout that met your eye when entering the show. A table just inside the entrance was a sight to behold. First was the fancy butter - beautiful roses and other flowers made in butter and sometimes farm animals. How long these must have taken to make, I do not know, or how they kept their shapes, was a mystery. So delicate and beautifully done, it must have taken many hours to do and in itself, was worth coming to the show to see.

Then the poultry, dressed of and ready for the oven. Huge turkeys over 30lbs., Indian game chicken 7 or 8lbs, ducks and geese. They made your mouth water.

A various selection of pot plants, i.e. cacti, chrysanthemums, orchids and cyclamen added variety and colour. The apples too were a wonderful sight, with their many colours - reds, greens, yellowish, brownish, russets. Five of each variety had to look like peas in a pod for shape and size and colour.

Then there was farmhouse butter in half-pound blocks. Bowls of cream, bottled fruit, raspberries, plums, pears, etc. Home-made jams, cakes and sponges. Plates of a dozen eggs, free-range in those days. This part of the show was nicknamed 'Farmers Wives Corner'.

Then all the root classes, i.e. swedes, turnips, mangels, flat pools (cattle cabbage). These were shown in groups of six and, again, had to match in size and colour. The cattle cabbages were shown in threes, and one often weighed between 40lbs to 50lbs, some more.

The cattle (no continentals) i.e. Belgium Blue, Charolais or Simmentals, but good old English and Scottish breeds, i.e. Ruby Red, Devons, South Devons, Hereford and Aberdeen Angus. The meat from these breeds was succulent, tender and very tasty, unlike the hard and, by comparison, tasteless beef of today.

The sheep were Devon Closewool, Devon Longwool, Exmoor Horn and Dorset Down. The meat from these, although tasty, would be too fat for the modern trade.

In the evening the South Molton Brass Band would play and the market would be packed with people. I believe the cost of entry was two shillings, and after 6 o'clock, one shilling. Sadly, as time went on, support dropped and although we kept going for a number of years, things became so desperate that the only way to keep going was to amalgamate with the Dairy Show. This we did, and renamed it the North Devon Autumn Show. This show has left its home in the Pannier Market and is now held in the Cattle Market, much smaller but still hanging on.

POLITICS

I still had a keen interest in politics and was loyally backed by May, as it meant many evenings out. I was Chairman of the Bishops Tawton Branch for many years. In the early sixties, when John was now home on the farm, I was persuaded to take on the Chairmanship of North Devon, a job I enjoyed. Jeremy Thorpe, the Liberal Leader, was M.P. for North Devon with a majority of over 5,000. A daunting task to try and win the seat. During the election he appeared on the T.V. each morning, a great advantage as his face was well known in North Devon. I must say, we had a most wonderful Conservative Agent at that time. He was a very great help to me, and often worked long into the night. A great personality, whom everyone liked. Unfortunately, he took too much upon himself and went down with the flu ten days before the election. We reduced Thorpes majority to 227 - a great achievement. If Derek, the Agent, had not gone down with the flu, I think we would have found those extra votes, and won.

Perhaps it is fair to state that Derek and I were a great team. It's not often that I blow my own trumpet but feel, in this case, I am allowed to do so. We worked ceaselessly in getting sixty-odd branches in fighting form, ready for an election whenever it came. We both had a terrific sense of humour and a knack of being able to chat people up and get their help, which we so badly needed. This often meant two or three nights a week at different branch functions, A.G.M.'s, etc. We had great fun and so much laughter in between the hard work. We made so many friends and met a lot of nice people. May helped me greatly and was a very loyal supporter of everything I did.

Despite our busy times, we still managed to re-build the old wooden building at the back of our Conservative offices. Thanks to help from many sources, it was now up-to-date: a hall on the lower floor seating 120 plus, a kitchen and toilets. Upstairs was a large committee room, and various smaller rooms for storage. It was now a real asset whereas before, it was a rather tumbled-down ruin.

Perhaps the greatest compliment I have ever received, was a few weeks ago when I met some people who were deeply involved with the Party, when Derek was an Agent and I was the Chairman. The words they used were: 'If only we could turn the clock back. We could have you as our Chairman and Derek as our Agent, then things would be good again, just like they were so long ago'. My reply: 'It's different days now.'

I suppose Jeremy Thorpe and I were almost enemies in those days. Time mellowed both of us and when sometimes we met, 35 years later, we met almost as friends.

During my term of office I had the pleasure of chairing meeting for two Prime Ministers: Edward Heath and Sir Alec Douglas Hume, and a future Prime Minister, Maggie Thatcher. Quite an honour. I suppose I attended four Party Conferences, and spoke at one on agriculture. In retiring as Chairman after five years, I was made President, an office I held for another five years after which, for my services to the Association, they made me an Honorary Life Vice-President. They also made me a Trustee of the Association.

I also had many happy years with the Conservative Club, and was their President for ten

May and Mrs Thatcher, when Prime Minister.

years and Trustee for twenty-five. I was made Life Member some six years ago.

I still take great interest in both the Club and Association, they both hold very pleasant memories of by-gone days.

When I first took interest in the Conservative Club, it was pretty run down in the early fifties. It did not seem to have recovered from the war years.

I, personally, had not been a member for years (just lapsed) but thought it was time I showed some interest, and joined again. It was not long before they asked me to fill a vacancy on their committee which I did, hoping that in some ways I could be of help. To say the least, their financial plight was pretty desperate. Every penny had to be carefully watched.

I managed to get some twenty people to become members - many of whom were May's family. A Ladies Committee was set up. They ran

The author receives a presentation of a set of golf clubs at the end of five years as Chairman of the North Devon Conservative Association.

Champions of Champions of the Barnstaple Skittle league, the author far right.

jumble sales and held dances in the ballroom, upstairs, and held small draws. They furnished the ladies toilets and powder room, and raised quite a bit of money. They are too numerous to name and, sadly, many are not with us any more but the club owes them a great debt of gratitude. They were there in time of great need.

I formed a skittle team called, 'Bert's Certs'. I don't know why? They were a great bunch of lads. We won many divisions in the Barnstaple Skittle League and coveted the Champion of Champions Cup. We also formed the Barnstaple Branch of the 'Enterprising Young Tories', (male and female). They met at the club and were a great help at election times and in raising money for charities. They offered to paint the ballroom (which had a sprung floor that you could feel moving when dancing on it) and which was in a rather shabby condition. I put this idea to the Club Committee, who were divided on what they should do. Some thought that, as amateurs, they would not do a good job. I was a bit doubtful myself. Any rate, after much discussion the go-ahead was given. The club would purchase the paint and hire a professional decorator to do the high ceiling. The B.B.E.Y.T. could do windows, walls, radiators, doors, etc. The ballroom was some twenty-four feet wide and sixty feet long. On the walls, some of the recesses had arches with fancy plaster decorations. Quite an undertaking. The paint was bought, the ballroom closed, the work was to begin - it lasted three weeks. Most evenings, after work, eight or ten people would turn up and spend the evening painting or cleaning, sandpapering wood, etc. They were a happy band. They did a marvellous job. The walls were blue and the plaster decorations were in gold, with the doors painted white.

We had a grand opening night - a Dance and Buffet. They, the Enterprising Young Tories (E.Y.T.), could be very satisfied with the work they had done. We now had a ballroom they could be very proud of, thanks to their efforts and skill as decorators.

From that time onwards, things bucked up and membership started to increase.

Somewhere about this time, fruit machines came into being. We had two in the club; one in the 'Men Only' bar and one in the lounge, where both sexes could drink and mingle. They were straightforward machines, (sixpence a time, jackpots £3 or £4) and gave many people lots of fun - to others who became obsessed with them, spent more than they could afford - a proper curse. The machines belonged to a machine dealer, who was responsible for the upkeep. The income was shared fifty-fifty with the club. A good investment for the owner and not too bad for the club, as we were taking an average £60 a week out of the machines.

It seemed to me that it would be a good idea if we could raise enough money to buy the £120 machine, thus keeping the whole of the takings. I raised this with the committee, who thought it a good idea to purchase two machines - but where was the £240 coming from. We were still living hand-to-mouth, with not a penny to spare. In the end I got them to agree, that if I could raise the money I could go ahead. I managed to get twenty-four members and friends to invest £10 each, interest free. Their names would go in a hat, and each week two would get their money back. In twelve weeks they were paid off and the Club owned the machines.

From those days on, the Club never looked back and is very prosperous today. Thanks to the ladies who worked so hard, the E.Y.T. for painting the ballroom and the people who lent their tenners. They all saw the club through its bad times.

I served, at different times, on Bishops Tawton Parish Council and served a term as District Councillor for Bishops Tawton and Athrington. I did not stand for re-election, for family reasons, which meant I was back in charge of the farm once again. I had not the time to do my job properly, if re-elected to the District Council.

MY DREAM AT LAST

With help from Dad, I at last realised my dream. A playing field for the children of Bishops Tawton, in memory of all those of this parish who gave their lives in the war 1939-45. The problem was a septic tank in one corner of the field. We could not open until the mains sewerage problem was solved, some three years later. In the meantime, we had raised a considerable sum of money (in those days) with bingo, whist drives and draws, so we had some £800.00 to invest in equipment such as slides, swings, roundabouts, large railway engine and vaulting frame. We also tarmaced and levelled pieces of the field to erect the above on.

We thought it would be nice if the plaque said, 'The Stanley Verney Playing Field in Memory of All Those of This Parish Who Gave Their Lives in The War 1939-45'. It was opened by Charles Chichester of Hall who had, himself, served in the war. We had stalls and a tea tent, all sorts of side-shows. Most of the village turned out and a great time was had by all.

After many years of disappointment and obstacles, I had fulfilled my pledge that my first priority was a playing field for the kids.

LEISURE TIME

John had been born in 1947. He still was our only child. We had hoped to have had at least two more children by this time. We had both sought medical help and taken many tests, but they could

Above, left and right. The opening ceremony for the Stanley Verney children's playing field at Bishops Tawton, and the celebrations and events that followed.

find no reasons why we had not increased our family. I think this was the biggest disappointment in our lives - this was to be disproved later on.

John, meanwhile, was now home on the farm. My right-hand man, which gave me a bit more time for recreation and passtimes. My father, until his retirement, had not had time for much recreation but was now a keen bowler and fisherman. He taught me how to fly-fish for trout and how to fly-fish and spin for salmon. I spent many happy hours on his beat at Halsdon, Dolton on the River Torridge, which had one of the best pools on the Torridge in its stretch of water, Golden Pool. The beat was 1.5 miles in length along one bank. Sea trout, salmon and brown trout were there in great numbers. He never kept records, but must have caught well over 200 salmon. I caught some 100, my record day being four in two hours. He also taught his grandson, and they often left at nine in the morning returning sometime in the evening. They had a great respect and liking for each other. John's greatest achievement was five salmon in a day and 54lbs. in weight of sea trout. His heaviest fish was a freshly run cock salmon of 25lbs. With me fishing with one rod in hourly spells, we bagged 56 sea trout. There were plenty of fish in those days and we had some wonderful days I shall never forget. Perhaps not a record to be proud of?

A record catch: 54 pounds of sea trout and salmon in a single day's fishing at Halsdon.

A spectacular catch - the family look on with pride.

When the fish would not bite, you could sit on the bank and watch the sand martins in the bank opposite, where they had their nest in holes. Often we'd see a beautiful kingfisher flying down the river. The mallard with their brood of ducklings, the buzzard hawks gliding overhead. The busy wild bees which for years lived in a hole in a huge beech, and on two occasions I saw the nearly extinct otter. A pair each time, playing in a deep, still pool well-shaded by trees. Then there was the woods behind, with magnificent oaks, beech and a pair of Scots pine which three people (with arms outstretched) might have just encompassed their huge girth, standing some 120ft. high. A truly handsome pair of trees. The fishing hut, where one could doze in a broken-down and very delapidated whicker chair, had a few books and magazines on fishing and country life. So, if you had a period of heavy rain, you could sit and doze in the dry or read, if you wished.

LEAVE THE COUNTRYSIDE TO COUNTRY PEOPLE

Some people, not understanding what they were doing, released a lot of mink in the wilds of North Devon. They soon found their way to the rivers where they did untold damage to birds and fish stock. A mink kills for the sake of killing, not because it is hungry. I had to watch, one day, the bank where the sand martins had nested for years. A mink went up the entire bank entering every nest and killing all the birds inside. I wonder what the people who released them in the wilds would have thought, perhaps they would have been proud of their achievements. My advice to people who do not understand country life and its ways, is to leave well alone.

Looking around our beautiful countryside, I think you must agree we country folk have not done too badly in maintaining habitats and havens for wildlife. Let things be, and don't try to interfere in something you know so little about, or the end results could be disasterous. Perhaps I should add, that since that mink destroyed the sand martins and their nests, I have not seen any sign of a sand martin there since. Let this be a warning to all the do-gooders, 'Look Before You Leap'. Get advice from country people, who know what is good for country life.

SHOOTING

Next, let's have a quick look at my other country sport - shooting and working my dogs. I think the greatest pleasure was working the dogs, and not the actual shooting. For the most part, the shooting was not of reared birds but wild birds hatched in the wild. I preferred a day of rough shooting (wild birds) mallard, teal, woodcock, snipe, pheasant, rabbits, hare and pigeons.

Shooting days. The author by the pond at Bellworthy in beautiful countryside.

Perhaps five or six guns would bag 20-25 head of game mentioned above, and would have walked maybe five to six miles in doing so. I enjoyed the company and the fresh ground you often shot over, more than the size of the bag at the end of the day.

Later on in life, I belonged to two small syndicates where we put down about 800 birds, of whch we shot in the region of 350 to 400. Where the rest disappeared, I do not know, but these figures were regarded as good. In this type of shooting you, and the guns, stood at the pegs numbered one to eight, the number of guns in the shoot. A team of beaters were employed to go in the wood or field of roots, kale, swedes, rape, at the far end, to drive the birds over the guns which were waiting at the near end of their beat. You were often waiting for very long periods, doing nothing, using this system. The bag was somewhere in the region of 45 to 60 for the day. Although the bag was larger, you could not work your dog except to retrieve. You were very limited in what you were all allowed to do. If you want to go shooting without too much effort, you should join a syndicate but if you prefer to work your dog and enjoy a good hard slog, not knowing what you will find, then rough shooting is what you require. To me, rough shooting will always be my favourite way of shooting. One wild bird is worth ten keeper-reared birds. As for the syndicates who put down thousands of birds, (where anything between 400 to 600 birds are shot in a day), I consider this to be mass murder, not sport, killing just for the sake of killing.

This is very briefly my views and thoughts on shooting. The sport which has given me lots of pleasure and in which I have met people of all walks of life, and made a great many friends.

GOLF

The other sport, which I took up much later in life, was golf. I only started playing because there were no longer any rabbiting parties, as myxomatosis had wiped out the rabbit population.

I never was a very good golfer, the lowest handicap i ever had was l8 shots. I never won any club cups but did once get to the final of two. I did manage to win quite a number of prizes in other competitions.

I am afraid I enjoyed the walk and the back-chat side far more, than the serious side of golf. Perhaps also, the cards, snooker and the odd drink or two at the bar, the idle chatter, and the leg-pulling that goes on, help make up for the silence on the course. I can claim to have had 'holes-in-one' on three occasions, so perhaps I was a reasonable golfer at one time, or dead lucky. There again, I have made lots of fresh friends, people whom I would never have met if I had not played golf.

After suffering two heart-attacks, I am no longer able to fish or shoot but with the aid of a 'buggy', am able to get around the golf course. As to how well I play, please don't ask. So perhaps, after all, it was a good idea taking up golf. At least it is something I can do with my friends.

May and John with a prizewinning trio at North Devon Show.

CHAPTER TWELVE
OUR FIRST COMBINE

In the early Sixties we bought our first Combine, a second-hand Massey 726 bagger machine. I say we, because I shared it with my two Brothers-in-law. The total acreage of corn grown by the three of us was about 170 acres; at about an acre an hour, some 150 hours work. Between us we kept the Combine running all day, no stopping for lunch or tea. We did some nine to ten hours a day if the weather was fine, some 70 acres a week, about two-and-a-half weeks work in all. I remember one year, having finished our own harvest early, we took on a few acres on a friend's farm. The farmer's wife brought out our tea and we told her to put it in the hedge, as it was a little early. We decided we would do one more round and then have our tea. What a mistake this turned out to be. A sow had come into the field, smelt the tea in the basket, and had eaten all the food leaving just the thermos of tea and cups. We were rather hungry when we arrived home that night!

CHANGES IN MY FARMING

For a number of years, from the early fifties, we supplied sterling chicks with hatching eggs. This meant keeping pure Rhode Islands and crossing with Leghorn cockerels. It was not quite as easy as that, as all the stock had to be 'blood tested'. This meant that if any failed, you had to find the bird with that ring number and remove it from the flock. Not an easy job, as hens were in 250 lots. Sometimes you were lucky, sometimes not. We also built a piggery to hold 120 pigs, which we kept to produce bacon and were sold to Harris of Totnes.

The cattle side of farming had changed from beef to dairy. A Guernsey herd was now in being. The milk we sold to a local factory, with a premium of 12 old pence per gallon, because of high butter fat. We started with sending 25 gallons a day, but in two-and-a-half years had increased to 100 gallons a day. We now had a milking machine and parlour, milking four cows at the same time. It took little longer to milk 100 gallons this way than it took to milk four gallons, by hand, the old way.

The pedigree Devons had now all gone, rather sad but a sign of the times. So now we had a large number of hens supplying hatching eggs, a piggery producing bacon and a Guernsey herd producing milk. A rather different set-up than the one I started my farming career with.

CHAPTER THIRTEEN
TWENTY YEARS AS A J.P.

Perhaps I should mention, in passing, that I sat on The Barnstaple Bench for nearly twenty years. I remember when I first sat, the ladies all wore hats - very smart - and carried or wore gloves. I think that no one can say that they enjoyed their years on the Bench. I don't think anyone can enjoy sending people to prison, which often is the only suitable punishment. Or fining people, when you know that innocent children will get no goodies at Christmas because of the fines imposed on a parent. It is a very difficult job to do and the public, sometimes with good reason, think we are too soft, which sometimes I know we are, but perhaps at other times we are too harsh. We can only do what we believe is right. We have to live with the decisions we make, so we try to get it right. Not easy. Remember that when giving punishment, in many cases, we have had the benefit of a report on the defendants background. Often, that background is largely responsible for their crimes. These reports, by the Probation Services, are very helpful and cast a very different view on the case. So perhaps, at times when you think us completely mad, there are very good reasons for doing what we did.

I found my term on the Bench interesting, but not enjoyable. One incident which still sticks in my mind is of a man (a lodger) who was accused of indecently assaulting his landlady. It came out in evidence, that they were sitting on the settee watching the television, when she felt a hand under her skirt, stroking her thigh. When asked, by the Chairman of the Bench, what programme she was watching at the time, the reply came back, 'Opportunity Knocks'. Titters came from everyone in court. But these funny moments were few and far between. You did your best to be fair to everyone, and could only hope that the decisions you made, were right.

During the time I spent sitting as a J.P., the questions that I was often asked were, 'Did I believe that the death penalty should be reintroduced and should corporal punishment be used in certain cases?' After much thought, the conclusion of my thoughts were, 'Yes. In certain circumstances the death penalty should be used'. The deliberate shooting or killing in any way of police or anyone else who was trying to prevent a crime. Where mugging and physical beatings has caused the death of innocent victims and where murder had been cleverly planned - yes. When done in a fit of temper, to be bitterly regretted afterwards, then life (meaning at least twenty years) may fit the bill. I think that the truthful answer to these questions can be found if you ask yourself: 'Would you be prepared to sit and pass sentence. Could you condemn a person to die?' If so, then I believe your answer must be, 'yes'. If it is all right for someone else and not you to make that decision, then your answer must be, 'no'.

With regards to capital punishment. Yes, I would like it to be used on certain people who had committed certain types of crime. Especially if someone had been mugged, thrown to the ground and beaten up or if somebody has been brutally attacked in their home, (and we do hear of some very brutal cases) where people have been left in great pain and shock. I think that the thugs that committed these crimes deserve to suffer pain themselves and I would have no qualms about ordering the birch in these cases. Six strokes now and six to be deferred, so that if ever they committed this type of crime again, they would know what their punishment would be.

The do-gooders have had their way for a long time - it has not worked. If one has to be brutal, then sadly, brutal we must be. Then, and only then, will it be safe to walk the streets at night. It is the general public who need protecting - not the thugs!

CHAPTER FOURTEEN
FARM ACCIDENTS

I was lucky that, during my time in farming, no accidents occurred which could have been fatal. I was very lucky indeed when helping to clear hay which had wound around the roller on the Allis Chalmers round baler. The hay was picked from the ground and carried to the bale chamber, on a short elevator, where it passed between two rollers into a chamber itself where fast-revolving rubber belts turned it into a round bale. Just like a rolled-up carpet - very neat, tidy and waterproof. The one snag being, that the tractor had to be knocked out of gear while the bale was being wrapped with cord. The elevated hay, entering the chamber, would have stopped. The power take off, driving the baler, was kept in gear. The driver, having knocked the tractor out of gear, was holding the power-take-off on the clutch. Suddenly, he released the clutch in a matter of a split second, my arm was in the bale chamber right up to my shoulder, in another one hundredth of a second and it would have been torn from my body. He must have heard the baler start up, and on hearing my scream, he banged his foot on the clutch and the belts and rollers stopped, leaving me trapped between two rollers. My arm was somewhere within the bale chamber but at what angle, I did not know, and what damage had been done, I did not know. Panic reigned, then someone said 'release the nuts', which put pressure on the rollers on my arm. It hurt like hell, but luckily they were hard rubber rollers with a bit of give, otherwise every bone in my hand and arm would have been broken. Having taken some of the pressure off my arm by releasing pressure at the top of the roller, someone realised that there was a reverse gear lever somewhere on the baler. The only way to release it quickly was to gently engage reverse gear, hoping my arm would find its way out without causing more damage, otherwise half the baler would have to be taken apart to get out the rollers and open up the bale chamber. I told them to put the machine in reverse and get on with it. I could not stick the pain in my arm any longer. The look on the staff's faces, was of horror, not knowing what would come out. The baler was put in reverse, the clutch released very slowly but surely, and slowly the arm came out of the chamber and the grip of the rollers. Everything felt O.K. but as my arm was still numb, I hoped that everything really was. I sat on the ground and could not stop trembling. The shock was coming out and after some minutes, and feeling no worse, decided I was fit to drive the car and go home. The arm, although badly bruised, had nothing broken. How it could possibly have been at that angle without breaking any bones, was a miracle. No one could believe that it came out only bruised. It must have been my lucky day.

CHAPTER FIFTEEN
NO ADDITIONS TO THE FAMILY

By the late Fifties, May and I realised that our chances of adding further members to our family was not going to happen. We both decided to take further tests to see if something had been missed. The results were the same: there was no reason why we should not have children. We thought of adopting, but as John was now twelve years old they would not be much use to him nor him to them. The age gap would mean that they would never be company for one another, so we decided against it. If we had known earlier, we would definitely have adopted one or two, so that all concerned could have grown up together and been company for each other.

A VISIT TO THE PALACE

Some time in 1970 we were invited to Buckingham Palace to a Garden Party. I don't know what I had done to deserve this invitation but I know May, a great Royalist, was really excited at the thought of going there and seeing members of the Royal Family at close range. It was a boiling hot day in mid-July, a day when toppers and tails seemed hardly the right dress for the weather. They were right for the occasion, so, toppers and tails it was. We went by rail, arriving in London about midday. We had lunch in St James Palace Hotel after which I donned topper and tails and set off for the Palace. We showed our passes at the gate and were escorted through the Palace to the gardens beyond. There, three huge marquees were erected with chairs and tables, on which you had your tea. We teamed up with an American judge and his wife, who were very gee'd up and excited at being invited to the tea party, and at the prospect of seeing most of the Royal Family. They deemed it the greatest day of their life. And when later, the Queen, the Duke, Prince Charles, Princess Margaret and Princess Ann appeared and mingled with the crowd, like May, they could hardly control their excitement. When talking later on about his job as judge in America, which I found very interesting. I found there was a little difference from what we do in this country. A judge in America always sits on his own, whereas here, in the County Courts, judges usually have two magistrates sitting with them. One thing he could not believe, was that magistrates were not paid for sitting in court and only claimed a meal allowance, if sitting all day, and a basic travel allowance. He wanted me to promise I would visit him back home, in America. I said 'One day perhaps', but never got around to it because of circumstances beyond my control. Rather sad really, I should have liked to have gone. May was thrilled with her day and has a couple of small pebbles from one of the many paths in the gardens, to remind her. It was a great spectacle - a happy and regal experience.

A truly memorable and happy day at Buckingham Palace.

SAD DAYS

My Mother and May's parents died during this period. Mother lived to see John married in 1970, and then seemed to give up. Her hard-working life, and the time spent looking after her daughter, finally caught up with her and she died in her sleep, at the grand age of eighty-five. She had been a great Mum to us all. We would greatly miss her caring and generous nature.

JOHN'S MARRIAGE

John was married to Diana, a garage and agricultural contractor's daughter. Very capable and nice girl. May and I both approved. Her father had a severe heart-attack while in bed asleep, and in a few minutes was dead. What a shock to Diana and her Mum. Diana left her job at the beauty salon in Exeter, and came home. There were petrol pumps and a shop attached to the garage. The agricultural contractors machinery was sold and that side of the business closed. Diana, like John, was an only child. They got married in the month we visited Buckingham Palace, July 1970. About 100 people attended the wedding. The reception was held at Dad's old school, Wallingbrook Hall. They spent their honeymoon touring Scotland.

When they returned, John took over the farm and stock, and was now in charge. I retained about forty acres of off-ground, which I owned, and kept some ewes and lambs. I was far too young to retire completely, so helped John at busy times on the farm and had the four holiday cottages to deal with. So I still had a very busy life. May did all the bookings, I kept the gardens tidy - cut the lawns, took the rubbish to the pick-up spot, kept the outsides painted and helped decorate the insides that needed to be done, during the winter. May organised all the cleaning and changing of the linen, with the help of a lady from the village.

Perhaps I should tell you, that before John and Diana were married, we all decided that it would be a good idea if May and I built on a wing to the existing house. Also, to take over two rooms of the old house, leaving them with three large rooms downstairs, an office, the old dairy. Five bedrooms and a bathroom upstairs, two loos (one downstairs and one upstairs). The dividing could be done by blocking one door upstairs and two downstairs, leaving two entirely separate houses. Although I had some misgivings as to how it would work, I was proved wrong, and we had a very happy relationship. We never fell out. We respected their side and they respected ours. In the end, it proved to be a blessing.

It was decided that we shared the garden and lawns. This worked like a treat, as neither John nor Diana were very keen gardeners. They were quite content for May to plan the planting and to

Overton where John and Diana joined us, showing part of the wonderful garden there.

keep the flower beds, rockery and shrubbery tidy and flourishing, and for me to keep the lawns cut.

John was now the farmer, his own boss, just like I was twenty-five years ago. All on the farm seemed to be going well. The Guernsey herd was doing exceptionally well, their milk records were excellent and all in the garden was lovely. The one blackspot was when Diana had a miscarriage. We were all disappointed, but in a short time she was pregnant again. This time everything was alright and she had, what May and I had always wanted, a baby girl. We were all so excited. We had never had the daughter we so badly wanted but at least we now had a grand-daughter. Life was good. Then, three years later on John's birthday, 10 April, they had a boy. So perhaps it had been right that I had stayed in farming. I had an excellent farmer, John, who now had a son of his own. Perhaps he would carry on the family farming tradition when he grew up. If so, my life would not have been wasted. All this would be a long time away, perhaps they would have more children. Anyway, they had no trouble with baby-sitters, they only had to ask and May was in her element to oblige.

TAPESTRIES

May and I were so pleased when John and his lovely wife, Diana, had a baby daughter, Lisa. May and I were 'over the moon'. We now had a grand-daughter to help make up for the daughter we never had.

May, during the previous year, had done a very lovely tapestry of 'The Last Supper'. She gave it to the church at Bishops Tawton, St John the Baptist, where it was dedicated and hung in the Ladies Chapel. We hope it will be there for many years to come, as a token of her thanks for a very lovely grand-daughter.

When Mark was born, some three years later, she had done another tapestry which hangs over the West Door, to show her thanks for a bouncing grandson. This time it was 'The Good Shepherd'.

May is very fond of her church, and seems to get a lot of help there in times of special need. She has rarely missed sitting in (what is known as) her seat, next to the font, and she has decorated this beautiful stone piece for Christmas, Easter, flower festival and other church festivities for the last fifty years.

We have many of her tapestries in our home - chairs, stools and tables with clear glass tops to protect the tapestries underneath. Many are hung on the walls. They really are beautiful pieces of work, which seem to improve with age.

Before we were married, May attended St Peter's, Fremington. We were later married there, on 5 September, 1945. She sang in the choir and is still remembered for her lovely voice, especially her rendering of 'I Know That My Redeemer Liveth', at Easter.

A Mrs Barclay-Black, (who was badly injured in a riding accident and had a period of nearly two years in hospital on her back) used this time to embroider curtains in silk, of flowers, which she gave to May for her wedding present. This she said was for the pleasure she had given her with her singing, at Fremington church. It had a place of honour at Overton for nearly fifty years. It was hung on a brass pole on the drawing-room door.

May has always enjoyed her church work and has strong beliefs of life eternal.

May as a choirgirl

CHAPTER SIXTEEN
THE SEVENTIES

It was now the late seventies. Lisa, John's daughter, started school at the Convent in Barnstaple. Mark, his son, was walking and talking. They were a lovely pair of children, we could be proud of them and their parents - we were a very happy family.

During the seventies, we had suffered badly from Dutch elm disease, and lost about sixty trees which left a huge scar on the countryside. Much beauty was now gone. To help repair this sad loss, John and I decided to plant some two and a half acres in three different plots with conifers and hardwood trees, oaks, ash, beech, red willows and weeping willows, and rowan (mountain ash). He also made three small ponds and stocked one with rainbow trout. I remember saying, as I was helping

John, Diana and their children Lisa and Mark.

with the planting, that I would not see the trees mature as I would be too old, but that John would, and think back on the the time when he planted them some 18 inches in height. He replied, that perhaps I would see them as mature trees and he would not. I told him not to talk so daft. These trees are now twenty feet tall.

Farming was changing once again. The milk, which had for years been collected in churns, would now be collected by bulk tankers. This meant that the milk on the farm had to be stored in a tank, cooled and sucked into tankers. Very nice and easy, no more heaving and lifting of ten gallon churns. But to John, the death knell for his Guernsey herd as the milk was mixed with Friesian milk, and could not be kept separate. He would only get the Friesian price and lose his 14p. per gallon premium. Although he struggled on for about three years the profit margin, without premium, was not high enough to make it worthwhile. The herd would have to be sold and many years of my work and all John's, to date, would now have to be cast aside. As his herd was one of the best in the South West, he had a marvellous sale. Purchasers from Scotland, Yorkshire and all over England came and he, as stated in the *Farmers Weekly* the following week, 'hit the jackpot'. Thus came the end of many years planning and hard work. The date of the sale was 14 October, 1977. The farming scene would now have to change again.

When my Mother died, the farm was left to me. I had to pay my sister a certain sum of money and two of the cottages were left to her, (which I later purchased). The farm was valued at a certain figure and death duties were paid on that figure which, in my opinion, was ridiculously low. I had a brainwave. I would immediately pass on the farm, at this figure, thus saving death duties at my death. This the tax people accepted, much to my surprise. John would pay me off over a period of years and have the farm for a tenth of its real value. He now not only farmed the farm but owned it as well. Something that I did for just a few days. He was well set up for life. A lovely wife, two happy and healthy children (a boy and a girl), and an occupation that he loved, farming.

In 1979 Father had a nasty tumble. The doctor sent him to hospital, as my sister would not be able to look after him until he recovered. It seemed minor at the time, and that he would soon be home. It was at the time of a General Election and District Council elections. Dad, a keen Conservative, was upset at not being able to vote, but at least he had something to read about and listen to on his radio. Maggie became Prime Minister, I won a seat on the District Council, Tony Speller won North Devon for the Conservatives. Dad was a very happy man. We were completely surprised to be called to the hospital at 11 o'clock at night, as they were very worried about Dad's condition. My sister, a friend and myself arrived at the hospital and were shown to a private ward, where Dad now was. He smiled and said how glad he was to see us. He quoted one of his favourite passages from the Bible: 'I shall go up into the hills from whence cometh my help.' He smiled again and was gone, up into those hills forever. A terrible shock to my sister and me, but a lovely and peaceful way for him to go.

May and I were now the older generation - it seemed rather strange but this was now the case. My memories of Dad - rather strict but a very fair man, whose family always came first. A good landlord, who had helped at least eight people to start their farming careers. He had deep religious beliefs. At 94, when he died, his brain was still very active. He still played Bridge at his Club and pottered a bit in his garden.

JOHN'S ILLNESS

Early one Sunday morning Diana came bursting into our bedroom. Would we come and see John, who had lapsed into a coma and was frothing at the mouth. The doctor soon arrived, and by this time John had stopped frothing at his mouth and was out of the coma, fit, or whatever it was. He, John, told us it was nothing to worry about as he had had these attacks before, and after a short while was normal again. He had not told anyone, as he thought we would be worried. The doctor said that many things could be the cause of this, and that he would like John to spend a day or two in hospital, where tests could be carried out to find the cause of these fits. I said that I could, with the help of a man, run the farm until John came home. Various tests took place and the results inconclusive. They decided to send him to Exeter, to have a scan of his head. He said that he thought they were making a fuss about nothing, and that he felt fine. Having received the results of the scan, they decided he would have to go to Plymouth to have a hole bored in his head to take a sample of the tissue within. By this time, we were pretty worried. So, off to Plymouth he went. The tissue sample revealed the worst fear, he had a cancerous tumour on his brain. It was of astral shape and could not be removed. If they tried there was not much hope of success and even if they could remove it, he would probably be a complete cabbage and not be able to speak, see or hear. We were completely shattered - our world had suddenly fallen apart. Our only child, Diana's husband, the grand-children's dad, was terminally ill with, at most, two years to live. We could do nothing to help but had to sit back and watch it slowly happen. What he, himself, must have felt at just thirty-four years old? A loving and lovely family, two children whom he would never see grown up. How bitter he must have felt and yet how brave and composed. He worried more about us - what a huge void in our lives at his going, how sour life had suddenly become. We asked ourselves 'Why?', and could find no answer. We had a very special relationship, John and I. We enjoyed so many things together. I suppose being an only child he turned to me, and he being our only child I turned to him. I, like many others during the war, had lost my brother whom I hero-worshipped. My best friend had died in a shooting accident, and now my son was being taken from me.

Life seemed very cruel to lose the three people who mattered so much and had such a lasting effect on my life. May and I had no other children to help ease the pain, we only had each other's shoulders to cry on, which we often did.

During John's illness, May was asked to open the church fete held at Tawton House. It gave her the opportunity to thank the people of Bishops Tawton for their help, and kindness to the whole family, at that time of very deep sadness.

It meant that I was now busy helping on the farm. John, when feeling well, drove the combine, planted corn, helped with lambing and kept the books. He even caught a couple of salmon and played the odd game of golf. He gave up shooting. He accepted his fate with courage and dignity. For the first year he showed no real signs of his illness, then after eighteen months he began to drag a leg. He soon needed the help of a stick as the tumour was affecting his senses and his body control. On Christmas day he was really poorly, he crawled down the stairs and lay on the carpet in front of the fire to be with his family, as we knew it would be the last Christmas with us all. His health slowly deteriorated and for his last few days, was in a coma. He had given orders that we were to get Diana a gold chain and cross for her birthday, 10 March, 1983. We gave it to her that morning and she wore it at his bedside. His eyes seemed to light up as if he knew, (perhaps it was our imagination) he sighed and then it was all over.

Diana had been very wonderful in the way she had nursed him and for the past fortnight had never left his bedside, only to do things that had to be done. She sat at his bedside and dozed at times in the armchair but was always there when needed, she could not have done more.

We shall never be able to thank Arthur and Clarice (May's brother and sister-in-law) enough - they arrived on our doorstep with suitcase in hand and stayed for a fortnight to comfort us.

I shall never forget the scene when we arrived at the church for the funeral - each side of the church, on the road, were hundreds of cars. The church was packed and people were standing outside.

We never knew that so many people cared. The letters that May and I received were overwhelming in numbers and contents, and the help we received from both our families.

About a month before John's death, he asked if I would promise him that I would carry on with the farm until Mark was old enough to know if he wished to become a farmer. I could not refuse this request but knew it would mean a full-time job for many years. May and I had hoped to visit members of her family in Australia and I wanted to trace relations in Canada. We had planned to retire completely and see a bit of the world. This was now not possible as I dared not leave the farm for long periods.

CHAPTER SEVENTEEN
BACK IN CHARGE OF THE FARM

We decided to have a sale to pay off a small overdraft and the small sum he still owed on the farm, and start with a clean sheet. This we did by selling surplus stock and machinery. We now had a complete change in the way we farmed the land. We let off 120 acres as grass keep, kept 130 acres for breeding ewes (which we would lamb in), grew a couple of fields of corn for straw and corn to feed the sheep. The combine did not sell in the sale, so we still had our own combine to deal with the corn. I managed with one man to run the show. We did not make a fortune by this system but we could keep our heads above water, pay the bills and the school fees which were now coming in - Lisa now at Edgehill and Mark at his dad's old School, Blundells.

I did not defend my seat at the District Council elections but if I had done, I think I should have had a free run and gone in unopposed. I would now be too busy on the farm to do my job properly. I had managed to help a few people during my period on the Council and quite enjoyed the job, and felt I was doing something useful. I still did a bit of shooting and played golf, when I had the time. I gave up the water on Dolton as it held too many memories. In fact, I gave up fishing as the desire was no longer there.

Mark showed no interest in any country sports and did not seem to be interested in anything to do with the country. As regards to being a farmer, he was not really interested. Lisa, on the other hand, was a different kettle of fish. She loved animals and helped with the lambing. She had a keen interest in horses and riding, and won many prizes at gymkhanas. She should have been the boy, if she had been, she would surely have been a farmer.

The years rolled on and we once again changed our farming, as sales of grass keep were not as good as in past years. We employed a very experienced farm-hand and gave him a pretty free hand.

We increased the livestock to 300 ewes, and bought in thirty calves a year which were sold for beef at two years of age. We made more hay and bag silage. We still let a few acres of off-ground for grass keep, but farmed the majority ourselves. We still had most of the machinery we needed. Any ploughing we contracted out, also hedge trimming.

I enjoyed helping at busy times but still found a bit of spare time to call my own, and could go with friends on golfing holidays abroad knowing that the farm was in safe hands, with no need to worry. This system was the last change we made in our ways, although we were very busy at lambing times. We now did this all indoors where it was warm and comfort-able, with everything you needed at hand - a simple job compared with my

Lisa riding in a gymkhana event.

first lambing outside, in 1937! We seldom lost any lambs at birth as they had some 12 - 24 hours in the dry and warm before they were put outside. In bad weather we could house about three day's lambs. I used to do the night shift, and enjoyed doing so. How good it felt to see the results of a night's work, sometimes as many as twenty or thirty lambs safely born, had all suckled mother and were fast asleep.

A good night's work well done.

TIME TO DECIDE

Mark was still at Blundell's and Lisa still at Edgehill. Mark was 13 years old and Lisa was 16. They were reaching the time of decision. Lisa wanted to join a firm of auctioneers and house agents. This she did and seemed quite happy in her work. I don't think she tried very hard at school, perhaps it would have been different if she had had a father. Diana tried to make up for the loss of their dad and was inclined to spoil them. She had a very difficult job to act as dad and mum and to help run the farm. We were hoping that she would have found someone to replace her great loss, someone she could spend the rest of her life with. Sadly, this did not happen and she is still alone, thirteen years on.

Meanwhile Mark, 14 years old, had made it quite clear that he wished to have nothing to do with farming. He would not even kill a mouse or any creature, so it was pretty obvious that with this attitude to life, farming was not for him.

The price of land and houses was falling. If the farm was to be sold, the quicker the better. His mother had a long chat with him and he said he could not send lambs and cattle for slaughter. He knew that this had to be done but wanted no part in it. I told him that I had hoped he would be a farmer and carry on the family tradition, but the decision was his. I would be disappointed but would understand. He told me he was sorry and knew how disappointed I would be but there was no way he was going to be a farmer. I suppose that my staying home in the war, to carry on the family tradition, had not exactly been wasted. John had thirty-five years of the life he loved, at least I had given him that. The home in which I was born and hoped to die in, was now on the market. The woods we had planted, the ponds, and May's beautiful garden, would soon be things of the past, just memories of happier days. I talked this over with my sister and May's brother. I wanted to be sure that it was right that Overton should be sold, as Mark was only 15 years old but certain he did not want to be a farmer. Was he too young and if so, at what age would he really know? They all knew Mark pretty well and agreed that as he disliked farming and its ways it would, under the circumstances, be wise to put the farm on the market as soon as possible. So that is what we did. Both Diana and Mark would be delighted to leave and live in Barnstaple. Lisa would miss her horse and the animals and I think, would have liked to stay. If only she had been a boy and Mark a girl, the family tradition would have carried on. It had been in the family for nearly ninety years, four generations had farmed it. It was going to be a wrench to leave it all behind, although farming was not my first choice as a career. The war made it impossible to do what I had set my heart on - it had been my home for sixty-nine years. I had been repaid as my son had so enjoyed life as a farmer. Why was his life so short? Why? Why? Why?

DECIDING ON SALE

A decision had been made and a great deal would now have to be done. It was time to decide which auctioneers and what the date of sale should be. Where to advertise and the setting up and printing of brochures. We decided to put it in the hands of two auctioneers, Kivells, and Gribble, Booth and Taylor, the firm Lisa was working for. We advertised widely with *Country Life*, *The Field* and many local papers. The brochure we produced was very good indeed. The farm and off-ground would be sold as a whole or in different lots. Everything collected over ninety years would have to be sorted out and put in lots, ready for sale. Three hundred breeding ewes to sort out, fifty beef cattle, fifty younger stock, sheep-handling and fencing equipment, feeding troughs, shearing machines, farm and barn machinery, miscellaneous farm and carpentry tools, oil tanks, chain saw, tractors, trailers, dung-spreaders, strimmers, garden cultivator, lawn mower and roller, swing hammock, garden seats and twelve stone troughs for garden flowers, surplus furniture, carpets, curtains, etc. So, although we had twelve weeks to get things sorted out, it would take all that time and there would be no time to spare. So much had to be done.

We decided to have the sale of stock on Wednesday, 19 September, 1990. The sale of the farm, cottages, off land and farm buildings for conversion, on 14 September at 2.30pm with possession on 15 October.

FINDING A NEW HOME

In the meantime, May and I went looking for a new home as did Diana, Lisa and Mark. After checking on many properties, May and I found only one which we both liked. About forty years old, built by a local builder for an architect and family, so was well built and only best materials used. It was in a good state of repair, and needed only woodwork done on one bow window. The kitchen needed gutting and refurnishing, central heating (gas) had to be installed and every room had to be redecorated. The house needed painting outside. The green-house in the garden, we knocked down, and rebuilt. The four cold-frames we dismantled. We enlarged the turning space outside the front of the house. When we opened up the garage at the side of the house, we found that although wide enough for a car to drive in, you had not got enough room to open the door. We then decided to turn it into a utility room, and had a wooden garage erected on part of the front lawn, against the boundary wall.

The sides of the house and back of the garden had high walls. The back wall was made of beautiful stone, being some twelve feet in height. The rear garden was completely private and could not be overlooked by neighbours. Against the wall were four lovely old-fashioned, scented roses, pear and apple trees. The view from the front of the house, about twelve feet higher than the road below, wasto distant hills, fields and trees. A friend and I completely redecorated the inside, when not busy on the farm and after the farm stock sale, a job which I enjoyed as it was going to be our new home. I could sit back and be proud of our work. We liked 'Verdala' so much, that I offered a price above the guide price. They would not accept, and I am glad they did not, because I bought it for £5,000 less at auction.

Sometimes 'a bird in the hand is worth two in the bush'!

We spent something like £9,500 in installing central heating, a downstairs shower, a completely new kitchen and rewiring throughout. We think we had a bargain. Although not like Overton, with its magnificent views, it was the best we could find. We hoped we would be very happy there.

My daughter-in-law and her family found a very nice bungalow about a mile away and have settled in well there. We are in easy reach of May's family and my sister.

LISA SELLS OVERTON

A week before the sale of Overton was due, we met in the auctioneer's office to discuss our chances on

Verdala - our new home.

the sale day. A great deal of interest had been shown in the lots of the land, but very little in the house. This was rather worrying as we had already bought our house and Diana had paid a deposit on hers. We only had seven days left and we did not want to have two houses on our hands. On the Saturday, Lisa said she was going to her office (although it was her day off). She said she had a feeling that she was going to get a buyer for Overton. We all hoped she would but thought the chances rather slim. A miracle happened. A man telephoned, saying he was looking for a large country property near Barnstaple, with a bit of land, where a horse could be kept. Lisa said that she thought she had a property on her books which might suit, where she thought people kept a horse, not letting on that the person who kept the horse was her, and the family selling the house were her grand-parents and mum. He asked where he could get a brochure and when could he view the property. She said that she would be in the office until six o'clock, if he could call. If not, she would put one in the post. He decided that as he was some twelve miles away and the time was 4.15pm, that he had time to call and collect it. He did, making an appointment to view on the Sunday at eleven o'clock. Lisa told him that great interest had been shown in the forthcoming sale of Overton. Her sales technique was correct except where the house was concerned - she was learning fast. When she came home, so excited, she gave us all new hope that a sale may be possible. The next day we sent her away to a friend's house, we did not wish him to know that the girl he had spoken to was involved in the sale of where she lived. To cut this short, he was very impressed and asked if he could bring his wife that afternoon, as she was coming down from Bristol. We said yes. She duly arrived, liked what she saw, asked roughly the guide price and agreed to meet the auctioneer in the morning. We kept our fingers crossed. We need not have worried. We agreed a price and the money was in the bank on Thursday. The house was withdrawn from sale on Friday, as we had already sold privately. Although we had to take £5,000 less than we hoped, it was sold and a great relief to us all. I gave Lisa a nice little present. If she had taken her time off on that Saturday, the buyer might not have known of the property up for sale.

Her thanks, some two months later, came when her firm started cutting down on staff - the last one in was the first one to go. As she was the last one employed, she was now out, not very encouraging for a young girl who had found the buyer for Overton.

The various blocks of land sold at pretty good prices, considering the trend of the market was downwards. Our farming days at Overton were now numbered. The stock sale in five days time, would bring the curtain down. The show would be over and only memories, some happy and some sad, would remain. We would be there a few more days, but the farm would be dead. No animals, no noise, just the breeze rustling the leaves on the trees. Some falling off and gently floating to the ground, their life ended too.

DIANA AND HER FAMILY

Meanwhile, Diana and her family moved to Sticklepath. They are a very close family. Diana still lives for her children and is still very proud of them. She, herself, now works for a firm of Solicitors, in Bideford. She likes the work and meets many people.

Lisa is now married, and seems content back at the job she loves, with an estate agent.

Mark seems mad on music (I wonder who he turns after)? Not ballads, but popular music. He is writing his own music, teaches the guitar and plays it in his group - which he has formed. They are now ready to go on the road. He is a very determined sort of chap and I am sure he will make a success of this rather strange career.

We have now been at Verdala for five years. May has transformed the garden and I have built a patio. We are snug and warm, the rush of life is past. We have time to sit, relax and dream of byegone days. May's health is still good. I have had a couple of heart-attacks but, with care, can do a bit here and there. I have had to give up shooting and fishing, as they are too tiring now, but manage to get around the golf course with the aid of a 'buggy'. I am rather short-tempered, and get very impatient and frustrated at not being able to do so many things. I should be grateful to May (my devoted wife) and my friends for looking after me so well.

NAN AND GEORGE

Before I end this book, I should like to pay a special tribute to a couple who were there when father was farming. They came in 1935 and were still going strong through most of my farming days, a period of thirty-five years.

Nan and George Matthews. They were chips off the old block, very true, loyal and reliable. I should think they were in their mid thirties when Dad employed him as horse-man, and she came to the house three mornings a week, to help.

She was always polite, just went on with her work in a quiet way. He was reliable and one could not find fault with his horse-work. How many thousands of miles he must have walked behind his horses - ploughing, working down, tilling - I would not know, but thousands it must have been, and worn out many pairs of boots.

They attended church on Sunday evenings. He went to the pub on Saturdays but never drank much, just the odd pint. He smoked a little, about twenty or thirty a week. Together they planted the vegetable garden. She was a good cook and manager, having served in domestic service before her marriage. They always had plenty of food. When Mother and Dad retired, she came to help May who was busy with the garden and poulty. When she discovered May was pregnant, she was so excited that you would have thought it was her. Unfortunately, they never had any children of their own. When May came back with the new-born baby, she had set out tea on the table and when May let her hold John, her joy was there for all to see.

I had Annie for my second Mum, and it looked as if history was repeating itself. John would have Nan, as he later called her, and so it turned out to be. When he reached the age of four or five, he would often go missing. At first we were very worried, but later found he had gone down to Nan's, his second home. He was safe there, so after a while this became a regular occurrence. Having never had a child of her own, this was the next best thing.

It was not long before he used to get out of bed at about 6 o'clock (he always was an early riser) and off he would go, down to Nan's for breakfast, and when George came to work at 7.30am, he would bring him back. Annie and me all over again! Then John started school - a day boy at first, so he only went visiting there at weekends and during the holidays.

There was far less horse work now, as we had two tractors, so we only kept one horse. George did a lot of jobs, carting odds and ends, brought in wood for firing and helped with bales at busy times. George, being an experienced farm-hand, could do most jobs on the farm. There were plenty of other jobs on the farm that he could do. He was a good hedge-layer and maker, so in the winter he spent quite a time at this. Also, carting hay and straw to lofts and yards. He was quite happy, and fully employed.

John was now at boarding school, so was only home on holidays. Nan used to write to him every week, telling all that was or that had happened on the farm. Then, when she was nearly sixty, she had a stroke which left her paralysed on her right side, especially her arm. She could not walk far, as her right leg was also badly affected. Not to be outdone, she learned to write with her left hand, telling John what she could see from her window. George was now nearing retirement age. He said he would like to work part-time. This suited me fine, as the horse was getting old too - it worked well both ways.

A few years later his one good eye (he only had one eye) gave up and he was blind. How would they manage? She badly crippled and he blind. Somehow, with home-help, they did. May or Diana used to buy their meat for Sundays and roast it at midday with vegetables and potatoes and some kind of sweet. I used to take it to them. They were so grateful. Life at times seems very cruel - she disabled, he blind. What had they done to deserve this? We told them that the cottage was theirs, rent free, for as long as they needed it. This took a great load off their minds, at least their home was safe. They had been good and faithful workers, now was our chance to give something back.

Nan, at times, fell out of bed. He could not get her back on his own, so we gave him a big hand bell. If in trouble, he would go outside his door and ring the bell until we heard, when we would go to his rescue. They were a grand old couple. They managed for another four years, then they could manage no more. They went to a home. We visited them regularly and they seemed reasonably happy. Nan had another stroke - this time fatal. He lasted a few months then, he too, found peace. A real old-fashioned, loyal and hard-working couple were at peace at last. What a sad ending.

George Matthews - a loyal worker.

Nan Matthews with John.

WHY I WROTE THIS BOOK

I only wrote this book to keep myself occupied. Whether it will ever be printed and published, I don't know. I hope, if it is, you will find it interesting in parts. Looking back, my whole life was decided by the spinning of that coin. It was marred by things out of my control. The death of my brother and my son. Now, after fifty years, May and I are still together. We have had some wonderful times. What lies ahead, we do not know, but one thing I think I can safely say is that I have not got an enemy in the world, and think that I never had one. 'It is better to say nothing, if you have nothing nice to say.' That has been my motto and it has served me well.

CHAPTER EIGHTEEN
THE CHANGES I HAVE SEEN

This chapter looks at some of the changes I have seen in farming practices during the last sixty years:

MILKING by hand in the twenties and early Thirties. Then by machine and bucket. The bucket, when full, put in a cooler then into churns. Then finally the parlour system, where eight cows couldbe milked at once. The milk then pumped to bulk tanks, cooled and picked up by tanker. No humping of heavy churns, from cow to tanker with no human effort.

CORN - first cut by binder (two men), stooked by three men, carted when dry by horse and cart. Two men in the field and one man taking the carts from the shed to the field. Two men in the yard, one pitching and one making ricks. (Handled at least five times).

THRESHING - eight or ten men. Today a combine harvester. Corn threshed in the field, one man, grain augered into grain trailer and taken to merchant or farm. Tipped in pit and augered to silos. All this done by machines. One man in the field, one man carting and augering the corn.

The straw baled by one man and tractor and baler. Big bales loaded by tractor - one man. Ricked by tractor - same man again. Untouched by hand. Modern combines can do two to three acres per hour - six or nine tons of grain.
The old way very manual.
The new way by machine.

CORN-WEEDING and WEED CONTROL - In the thirties corn-weeding took a very long time. In badly affected fields, up to a week using four men. Docks on the pasture, were dug by hand. Thistles were cut by sythe or machine to check but not to kill. Today, sprays are used and up to Ten acres an hour can be done. What this is doing to wildlife, I dare not think.

POTATOES - Dropped by hand then covered over by machines - a very laborious job. Today, they are planted by machine and three men - one driving the tractor and two dropping potatoes down a shoot into a trench made by the machine. Another device at the back of the machine, covers them up. Three or four acres a day can be done this way. The old way, with same number of men, half an acre. No back-ache now!

PLOUGHING - Horses in 1920 and early thirties covered one acre per day. Early tractors and ploughs covered five to eight acres per day. Modern four-wheel drive tractors, with five 'furrow ploughs', can plough some fifteen acres per day

Changes in the farming scene, Left: harvesting at May's family farm in the 1930s. Below: Combining at Overton in the 1980s.

and up to twenty on light soils. Working down is done by going over ground once. With the old way, with old machines, three or four times was needed.

DUNG and MANURE - The old way - the butt is filled by hand, taken to fields, unloaded in heaps by hand, then spread by hand. The modern way - loaded into dung-spreaders mechanically, spread by machine and untouched by hand!

TRANSPORT - Horse and trap. Then cars. No drovers in the market, now all were transported by huge cattle transporters, three-decks. Motorways, link roads, round-a-bouts, jet air travel, rockets to the moon, or a tunnel built joining England and France.

And in FACTORIES - Robots do the work of man on assembly lines. Computers do the work of many office staff. Plastics have largely replaced most tin.

The small, mixed Devon farm in the thirties, employing two or three men, is now run by just the farmer. Farm cottages have either been sold or let, to people who have nothing to do with farming. Thousands have lost their jobs on the assembly lines and many more by the introduction of computers and other time-saving devices.

The village shops, now all gone, unable to compete with supermarkets

The medical world today - heart and kidney transplants, key-hole surgery, use of laser beams, antibiotics, and scanners are some of the advances since I was a lad.

If this is progress - and surely it must be - it has been bought at a high price: 2,000,000 unemployed. In the thirties, the factories, farms and mines would have needed all these people to produce what we do today.

The countryside is still much the same. A few hedges gone here and there, but country LIFE has changed out of all recognition. The farm worker has disappeared - a very rare commodity these days. The bond that held all those that worked the land is no longer there. The farmers' wives and their stalls in Barnstaple Pannier Market are things of the past. The harvest festival at church and chapel has lost its meaning and only a few people attend, the friendship and strong community feeling. Now gone.

The countryside and the people I remember as a kid have gone too, replaced by the modern world which will itself be replaced by another, in the next generation. That is life! That is progress?

Above: May and my wedding. Left: Fifty years on!

Below: Our family.

A morning's bag at the Stag's Head in later years.

PART TWO

∽ SCRAGGY ∽
A TRIBUTE TO A REALY GREAT DOG

If you find these stories of Scraggy interesting, as I hope you will, you must thank Frank Thorne who persuaded me to write what I can remember of a great dog.

This is my tribute to Scraggy's ability. A dog whose stamina was inexhaustable, whose retrieving was unbelievable, whose hate of foxes and love for the donkey had to be seen to be believed, and the few fights he had will never be forgotten. After all this time, (thirty years), people still remember him. The smallest of the litter, so thin and small he never became big, but had a heart of a lion. He saw no danger, never faltered and only beaten in the end by some poison which he picked up somewhere. Even now, after all these years, the grass seems to be greener on HIS resting place beneath the oak (which was also his favourite place in the summer heat). Imagination? Perhaps so, perhaps not.

The little brown-and-white-Spaniel pup whimpered as he left his basket by the fire, and waddled slowly to where I was sitting, dozing. Curled at my feet, he looked up towards my face with eyes that seemed to say, 'Where am I? Where's my brother and sisters and my mum?' He had only arrived here that day, eight weeks old. No wonder the world seemed strange and sad to him, perhaps he wondered who I was, and what kind of master I would make?

I gazed down at him and as I stroked his head, my mind wandered back to the day when I first met the 'Fearless One'.

It all started one market day. We were discussing the hatching season, and how the heavy thunderstorms would affect the young birds who should be hatched or very near to doing so. I remember the beer that day tasted good; perhaps it was the very humid weather that gave one a good thirst, that seemed to make it taste extra special. The subject of conversation got around to shooting and gun dogs. My dog, Scampy, was getting on a bit and when we worked out his age, during the conversation, (eleven years), I said that I would not mind a pup to train with him. Whereupon a friend of mine, who had a good name for breeding dogs, said he had a litter at home - eight in all - and if I'd like to look down, I could take my pick, as they were about eight weeks old and just fit to wean.

We arranged the next evening. So, after tea, I jumped in the car and drove to my friend's farm which was on the other side of Barnstaple, about six miles beyond. An old-fashioned farm, stone built, solid, had withstood many Atlantic storms. On a clear day kept watch on Barnstaple Bar, the bay beyond and Lundy Island in the distance.

There was one custom carried on at the farm which was in keeping with the strongly built buildings - a cider press. This was still used every year, and the cider produced by those people was much sought after. In fact, they had so many friends call to see them, that above the Cider-House door was a sign 'The Dew Drop Inn'. It was to the Inn I was taken that evening - what a grand place! The wonderful smell of cider as you opened the door. About twenty barrels of various sizes stood down one side of the building. The huge slate stones which formed the floor were well worn and hollowed by unceasing foot-prints around the casks. Wooden benches ran down the other wall, an odd selection but matching the oak beams which ran shortwise across the ceiling, giving a homely, warm and becoming look.

We had to sample the cider, and I was beginning to wonder when I was going to see the pups. Dick must have guessed what I was thinking, for he gave a low whistle and from underneath the huge casks, at the far end, pups of all shapes and sizes appeared. Mother, father, two uncles and finally the pups. 'Take your choice,' Dick said, and I began to eye the pups. Seven pups with their proud mum and dad. 'But I thought you said there were eight, Dick?' At that very moment, number

The Dew Drop Inn

eight appeared - much smaller and scruffy-looking. Having missed the rest of the family, he wandered right up to where I was standing. He sat at my feet, tugged my trousers playfully, looked up to my face as if to say, 'Take me, I'm the one for you - I know I'm small and scruffy, but I'll grow and you won't regret having chosen me.'. By the time the others had wandered up to where we stood, Dick said, 'There now, take your choice. I should have told you seven and a half pups because the one by your feet, well, I don't know what I shall do with him, I think I ought to have had him put down, as I don't think he will ever make it.'

I stood there for a moment, looking down at the eight pups. The little one was still sat between my feet. I bent down, picked him up, turned to Dick and said, 'This one will do, I know he's small and scraggy but he has already learnt to fend for himself, and I bet he makes a good dog'.

'Well I'm damned,' Dick said, 'fancy picking that one. I haven't got the nerve to charge you for him, take him if you must, and if he is no good have another from the next litter.' I insisted on paying the same as asked for the first pick, and having passed across the money, picked up my bundle of skinny flesh and made off towards my car.

On the way, I bumped into two of Dick's sisters who had come to say 'good-bye' to the pup, and could hardly believe their eyes when they saw the specimen I had chosen. 'What are you going to call him?' they both asked. I had not really thought, but without hesitation I said, 'I think that "Scraggy" seems to fit him.' So, Scraggy it was.

The journey home was uneventful. When we arrived and I put Scraggy on the kitchen floor, my wife eyed him and said, 'He's not very fat, haven't they been feeding him? Are all the rest like him?' 'No,' I said. 'The rest are looking fine, but somehow I fancied this one. Give him three months and you won't know him.'

Scraggy did grow in the next six months, although he still remained very much on the rakish side. He was now thoroughly at home in his new surroundings. I suppose he got up to the usual puppy tricks, but nothing in particular sticks in my mind.

Unfortunately, my old gun dog had contracted hard pad during this time, and died. So, for the coming shooting season I was left with Scraggy, just a six-months old, immature and pretty backward - not a very encouraging prospect. A neighbour, knowing my predicament regarding my dog and knowing that he was new and untrained, came up one afternoon in early September to say he had three or four pheasants in his garden, and thought it may be a good idea if I brought Scraggy along to see what he made of them. I could see no harm in doing so and Scraggy, so far as I knew, had never seen or scented a bird in his short life. So, off we went.

Sure enough, three young cocks were in the corner of his garden and, on seeing Scraggy and me, disappeared in a small clump of brambles by a rather antique and very rusty wire fence. I took Scraggy to the spot where I had seen them go into the brambles, and as the clump was rather thin, I could see two of the pheasants nearly fully feathered, squatting down amongst the brambles and rough grass. I tried everything to make Scraggy interested in them, but he stood there with a look as if to say I was mad and showed not the slightest interest in the two squatting birds. They soon decided they had been stared at long enough and ran off along the fence, in full view of Scraggy and, much to my dismay, showed not the slightest response. Just one casual look and he turned away.

While this was happening, the other bird took

to the wing and flew across the truly beautiful Taw Valley to the safety of the woods, about 400 yards away. I turned to where Scraggy was rolling in the grass - he got up, wagged his tail, and stared towards the garden gate as it to say, 'Enough of this nonsense, come on, let's get home.' I turned and followed, and the owner of the garden said to me, 'Well, you have certainly got your hands full if you are going to make a dog of him.' By the interest he had shown, I had to admit, 'By God he's right, I think I have boobed this time in picking him.'

HIS FIRST SHOOTING SEASON

Some friends of mine had a rough shoot of some 700 acres, consisting of about half a dozen farms about twelve miles up the Taw Valley between the village of Chulmleigh and Winkleigh, where we used to go on seven or eight Saturdays during the season. We had been three or four times during September and October. The partridge had been fair, the pheasant not too bad and the mallard rather scarce.

It was now the end of November. We decided that as the woodcock and snipe would now be in, it would be worth another trip. As they knew I had this young pup, Scraggy, they suggested I brought him along. Thus began his shooting career! I agreed to give it a try, in the hope that the other dogs would encourage him to take some sort of interest in shooting, and what goes with it.

We set forth about 10am on a dull but quiet day. I kept well on the flanks with Scraggy, as it took me most of my time to make sure he did not disappear at the sound of a shot. At least after seven or eight shots he seemed to be getting over the shock of the bangs which the first few gave him, and once or twice put his nose to the ground and poked his nose in the hedge - either to get out of the rain (which was by now teeming down) or else just out of sheer curiosity.

At about 3pm we were all pretty wet, so we decided to pack it in, and I don't think there was anyone more happy than Scraggy at this decision. He was now thoroughly wet and looked skinnier than ever. I am sure if he could have spoken he would have said, 'Well, if this is shooting, you can keep it!' At least, by the very doleful look on his face, his sad eyes, that is what I think he felt.

As we were all so wet and muddy we decided, at least, to remove our shooting kit and put on a dry jacket before setting off for home. Then it happened. A van came around the corner just as Scraggy decided to cross the road. The screeching of brakes, water flying off the wet surface, a yelp of pain from Scraggy as the front wheel of the van hit him in the midriff and sent him flying into a very wet and muddy ditch. Flustered and shaken, the driver of the van wrenched open his door and stood in the pouring rain. He said how sorry he was to have hit the dog, who was now struggling out of the ditch, making the road (half crawling, half limping) towards me.

I think I went half-way to meet him, picked him up as gently as I could and carried him wimpering to the car and deposited him gently on the back seat. I turned to the driver of the van and told him that it was just 'one of those things', and that I did not consider him in any way to blame. He muttered something about, 'he hoped the dog was not too badly hurt, and that he would soon be O.K. again'. He jumped into his van, and with a look of relief of his face disappeared around the next bend.

My dry jacket was covered in mud and nearly wet through, but my thoughts were on how badly Scraggy was hurt, and the sooner I got him home and dried off, the better. I said a quick 'good-bye' to my friends, jumped into the car, gave that poor wretched mud-coated thing on the back seat a reassuring pat on the head, pressed the starter, engaged the gear and sped for home.

I don't think we were long making the journey home. Thinking back, I am sure that despite the waterlogged roads and teeming rain, we made the journey in record time.

I parked the car outside the door, gently picked up the wet and muddy mess from the back seat and carried him to his circular wicker basket, which I placed in front of the blazing fire. I had just time to take the towel from the roller on the door when May, my wife, came in. 'What have you done to that poor thing in the basket?' she asked. I quickly explained what had happened, whilst softly towelling the mud and water from the skinny body of a sad and shivering and muddy dog. After about a quarter of an hour, I managed to remove most of the mud and water and he began to look a bit more like a dog. Meanwhile, May had put a bowl of warm milk and a dish of chopped meat by his basket, but he had no wish for either. He just lay curled in the basket, with steam rising from his stil, wet body. An occasional shiver, a deep sigh, and all the time his doleful eyes staring nowhere.

We finished our supper and sat beside the fire. I lit my pipe, picked up the paper - I suppose I read for a while - and then dozed off into a deep sleep. I was awakened by May tapping my shoulder and saying that it was time for bed. I took a look at Scraggy; spoke a few soft words to him but got no real response, so I banked-up the fire, covered him with an old blanket, and decided I could do no more for him at present. Wondering what he would be like in the morning, I left the light burning and went up the winding staircase, to bed.

The next morning Scraggy looked much more like a dog. He had completely dried out. I took him outside for his morning turn-out and, although pretty stiff, seemed much better than the night before. On his return to the house, he ate a couple of chunks of meat and had a few laps of the water before, once again, curling up in his basket beside the fire. The next day, although still rather stiff and sore around the ribs, he ate his normal food. I knew he was on the road to recovery.

I don't think much more of real interest happened that season but, by the end of it, Scraggy was fully recovered and showed some interest in our shooting. He rose a couple of birds on his own! Perhaps it is right to state, that he failed to pick up a runner at the end of the season, although he showed a good deal of interest in trying to do so. I think, in all fairness to him, and to give you some idea of the kind of dog he turned out to be, I should try to tell you of some of the things which I shall always remember about him, which occured during the next eight years of his life.

MEMORIES OF BOXING DAY

On Boxing Day we usually had a family rough shoot at my wife's parents farm which I can see away in the west, about four miles distant. Across the Taw Valley, the woods of Tawstock Court are now bare and sullen in the grip of chill winter, 'neath the dull and windswept sky. The shoot bag for the day should be about three brace of pheasant, ten or twelve woodcock, eight or ten snipe, a dozen or so rabbits and twenty to twenty-five pigeons. The Guns would be my wife's three brothers and brother-in-law, Arthur, Fred, Roy and Stuart. Arthur, a great sportsman and optimist, who lived for his shooting and Fred, not quite so keen but he had a loud booming voice and a deep, hearty laugh. Frank, a neighbour, a very quiet retiring sort of bloke who never seemed to hurry, but got there in the end. Sometimes May's father joined in, if the weather was good. I should think he was a very good shot in his younger days, and he could still knock them down pretty well. Arthur's son, David, and my son, John, used at first to beat and later shoot with their 4.10s. It was great to see their eyes gleaming with excitement when they were first allowed to shoot, and then great joy and pride when they managed to shoot a bird.

There was Roy, May's eldest brother, and later his son John (who was page-boy at our wedding). Roy, a hard-working and successful farmer, was a rather quiet sort of chap but deep down kind and caring. He enjoyed his Boxing Days, to be with his family and later with the kids in the evening at his old family home. I think he enjoyed this part more than the days shooting.

Stuart, another member of the family, married May's sister, Frances. He served in the R.A.F. during the war, mostly as a photographer on reconnaissance over India and neighbouring countries. He thoroughly enjoyed his shooting, as did his son, Marcus, in later years. He was not a brilliant shot with the gun, but was unbeatable with the shots he took with his camera. First with R. L. Knight, and later in his own business, S. H. Bath. Many photographs in this book are his work. He also was a great family man.

Then there was another neighbour, another Frank, very keen, who enjoyed his shooting in a quiet sort of way. Then there was myself. Keen and happy if others had most of the shooting, enjoying the laughter, especially if you missed an easy bird and the general banter that went on all

A happy pair. John, aged 11, with Scraggy

day. It was great fun to see all the shooting accessories on show for the first time - Christmas presents included cartridge belts, shooting hats and jackets, game bags, shot counters, hip flasks, etc. It was also interesting to see what came out of the lunch-bags: goose-legs, Christmas pudding, mince pies and cream, oranges and apples. A bottle of whisky was passed around. You either had it in your coffee, or neat! It was a great sight, held in the true festive spirit.

The farm, of about three-hundred acres on rather wet, clay soil, had about sixty acres of rough, scrubby woods, ideal for woodcock. Twenty odd really wet acres, ideal for snipe. Wherever one went, one was likely to see game of one sort or another.

I remember one lunch-break in particular. We used to use an old barn, with bales of straw for seats and tables. The barn was very old, about ninety feet long, twenty-five feet wide and fifteen feet to eaves. Walls were of cob and stone and the roof, of tiles. It used to have an old barn thrasher one end and potatoes, corn and hay stored at the other.

On this particular day, we had nearly finished lunch and the dogs were enjoying the scraps thrown to them. Unfortunately, one of the scraps thrown landed on Scraggy's back. It was meant for a terrier, belonging to Frank. He made a dive for it and, in grabbing it, nipped Scraggy in his back. He did not take kindly to this and snapped back. In turn, incited the terrier who started a fight, much to his regret. Scraggy grabbed him by his throat and refused to let go, despite cuffing across his head and tugging at his collar and pinching his tail. We could not get him to release his grip. Luckily, someone had some hot coffee left and a cup poured over his nose, did the trick. I don't think that terrier will start a fight again. He well and truly had a lesson in good manners. Yet, despite the fracas, the two dogs were hunting together on the next beat, in and out of the rough, as if nothing had happened.

A DAY OUT WITH FRIENDS

Scraggy was much sought after by my friends, if they had a rough shoot and I could not be there. We had some shooting at Crediton, some thirty miles distant, consisting in all about two hundred acres of rough scrubland, some forestry land, etc. and a stream through the middle. There was a large house (used to house people who needed medical attention) surrounded by rather overgrown gardens. One had a job to tell where the garden ended and the rough began. A great shame, as the gardens must have been magnificent in bygone days, but ideal for rabbits and grey squirrels and woodcock.

It was a really hard slog to shoot this area. Very steep in places, very dense in others and the few fields left in the middle, very wet and heavy. The cows used to cross these fields daily, to a small field of kale by the big house, walking in oozy, smelly mud. This had to be crossed, to reach the small yard where the cars were parked at the end of a day's shooting.

As my friends were trampling, wearily, through the mud at the end of a hard day's shoot, (for man and dog alike), they were more than a little concerned with Scraggy. When crossing the last stretch of stinking mud, to reach the cars, he was left further and further behind. He seemed hardly to have the strength, or will, to make it to the cars. They were very worried indeed, as he was walking with his tail between his legs and a sad look in his eyes, as if doubtful if he would make the last few yards. They related all this to me, when they returned Scraggy, and were very worried for the wellbeing of the dog. They hoped he would buck-up and be fit and well in the morning. On hearing their account of what had occurred, a smile crossed my face. I told them not to worry, as I had seen Scraggy like that many times before. There was nothing wrong with him, it was just his way. He was not tired. 'Why are we stopping shooting?' He did not want to go home. He wanted to go on hunting. In fact, he was sulking!

Scraggy was now four years old, and was making quite a name for himself in his hunting and scenting abilities, and his brilliant record in retrieving. I think one of his best efforts occurred at a small rough shoot at Alswear. We arrived at the last coppice at about 3 o'clock on a warm, dull, windless day. The guns were placed around and

Scraggy and I were left to beat and drive out any birds, therein. We quickly flushed a woodcock which was shot by one of the wing guns. A cock pheasant rose and flew straight and fast ahead. A double-barrel was heard. I could not see, from where I stood, if it was dropped or missed. For the next three or four minutes Scraggy was having fun and games chasing a rabbit around the thicket, from one clump to the next and back again. He was finally persuaded to leave, and the rabbit made a break for it across the field, on his left side, where it was shot by the gun placed there. That completed the drive, and we emerged at the far end of the wood to where the gun was stood, who had fired at the cock pheasant. He told me he had winged the bird, which had then run into a hedge at the far end of the field, some four hundred yards distant. As it was quite a while ago, he did not think there was much chance of a dog getting scent or catching the bird. Anyhow, I said I would have a quick try, so I took the dog to where I was told the bird had dropped. Off Scraggy went, sniffing the ground to the far hedge. When he arrived there he went through the hedge, into a field of kale, and disappeared into the middle. I went no further, as I knew I could do no good. It was now up to the dog. I put down my gun and lit my pipe, quite happy to have a bit of a breather.

It had been a hard day - wet under- foot and humid over-head. Five minutes went by; no sign of the dog and no sound of his yap which he usually gave, when in close pursuit. Then, there it was, a couple of excited barks way beyond the field and deep in the wood on the other side. Then silence. After another long wait, the kale began to wave. Something was coming back across the field towards where I stood. Scraggy came out by the hedge and, in his mouth, was the cock pheasant, still alive. He came to me, and I took the pheasant from his mouth and put it out of its misery. We returned in triumph to the guns waiting at the end of the field, who promptly told me that we had been 'twenty minutes retrieving that bird!' The spot where he caught it, must have been at least half a mile from where it was brought down. The next week, although I was not there, something similar occurred.

A bird was dropped over the far hedge of a field. This time, Scraggy was away fifteen minutes before returning with the bird. This time the bird was dead. This feat so impressed one of the guest guns, that he wanted to know if the dog was for sale. Ray, my friend, said he did not think I would be very pleased if he returned with a fat cheque, and no dog! How right he was.

Looking back, I can only remember three birds he did not retrieve. Two in his first season and one in his last, when a crafty cock got in amongst some motes by a hedge. Scraggy was now too slow to catch the bird but, with his record, I think he could be forgiven. He was also an expert in the river, retrieving duck. Seeing his prey in the river, he would run down the bank and jump in and swim across, below the duck, and wait for the current to float the duck to where he was dog-paddling. Whereupon, he would gently pluck the duck from the water and return to the bank.

One day we nearly had a disaster. It was very, very cold weather, with very severe frost. The river itself, partly frozen, with ice extending out from the bank some four or five feet, in the calm water. Someone, I can't remember who, shot a duck which landed plump, in the middle of the river. Away went Scraggy. Unfortunately, the duck was not dead and dived under the ice on the bank below where we stood. Scraggy followed. We

Waiting for the off.

suddenly realised he was in grave danger of drowning. Luckily, there was a large pole on the bank which we grabbed and, after a few frantic blows, broke the ice and Scraggy was able to escape. Needless to say, we were all greatly relieved. That was the end of duck shooting that day.

There was possibly a fourth bird that he failed to retrieve. We were shooting at Filleigh, on a hill behind the pub, when a friend of Doc's brought down a cock pheasant. It fell some distance away, on another hill covered with fern, bramble and larch trees. It was some five minutes before Scraggy came back to me, he had been working the hill from whence the cock pheasant had risen. I sent him to the other hill to find and retrieve the bird. Off he went, and was gone some fifteen minutes with no sound or sign of him. The other guns were ready to do the next beat, so I told them to go on - I would follow when Scraggy came back. I was rather worried. Scraggy was now twelve years old, not as fast as he used to be but still a dog of great courage and stamina. There had been no yapping, which meant he was in hot pursuit. Very strange, could he have had a heart-attack and be lying up there in the hills? I had asked the beaters to keep an eye open for him. I had a strange feeling that all was not well. I waited another ten minutes or so, he still had not returned. I was sure now that something had happened to him, so I set off slowly up the hill to see if I could find him. I zig-zagged across the hill, covering as much ground as I could, and finally met guns at the far side. We decided that, as it was nearly time to return to the pub for lunch, we would spread out and walk back through the wood looking for him on the way. We had got about half-way, when someone shouted that they had found Scraggy. He was coming towards them from the first hill, where he had risen the pheasant. I was mighty relieved. My fears had come to nothing. A great feeling of relief swept through me, so much so that I did not think what Scraggy was trying to tell or show me. When we reached the place where I had sent him in search of the pheasant, (we were on a path) the spot where I had been standing was just over the hedge. He twice jumped on top of the hedge, and I called him back and told him not to be silly, we had already done that bit. We arrived at the pub and had lunch. The episode was soon forgotten.

The next week we were doing the same beats again, so we decided to do it in the same order as before. I would go with a couple of guns and they would stand, and I would work the hill with Scraggy. To reach the hill, I had to pass the spot where I had stood and sent Scraggy looking for the cock pheasant, the previous week. There, on the ground, were a heap of cock pheasant feathers. Where had they come from? What I believe had happened, was that Scraggy had retrieved the bird the week before, and brought it back to where I should have been waiting; but I had gone. I had never done that before. He had done his part - I had let him down. He would now have to find me. He was getting old and slower. Why had I not waited; didn't I trust him any more? I should have known that he would have come back to me, he always did. What was wrong with me? And why did I not allow him (on the way back to the pub) to go into the field where he had dropped pheasant, on the spot where I had been. In his mind I must have gone completely bonkers. He had done his job, why had I let him down? I shall never know if this was the case, but somehow I feel it was. So, although I can never prove that he retrieved that bird, it was a strange coincidence the feathers were on the spot where I had been standing, waiting. These being the facts, I am prepared to give him the benefit of the doubt. He had brought it back and I was not there. He had done his job. I had let him down.

※

On one of our beats at Alswear, there was a field with a donkey which I am sure waited for Scraggy. When crossing this field, the donkey would gallop towards us, braying as he came. Scraggy would run to meet him, and the donkey would then gallop around the field, kicking out his heels with Scraggy barking behind. This lasted about three minutes, then all would stop and peace would prevail once again, until the next shoot, when all would start once again. One day, while shooting in the area, someone wounded a fox which made it to a thicket, at the far end of the field. Along came Scraggy and made off in hot pursuit, disappearing into the thicket, from where the sounds of snarling and fighting started up. My son, John, who was with us that day (aged fourteen) and armed with a 4.10 jumped over the fence into the thicket only to find Scraggy, and the fox, with jaws interlocked, refusing to let go of one another. After a while, a brief pause came in the fighting and he was able to shoot the fox, and unlock their jaws. Scraggy had a hole in his skin, half way up his nose, where the fox's tusk tooth had gone right through.

Scraggy had a love/hate relationship with foxes. He really loved to hunt and chase them. At my old home, at Overton, one year in the early sixties, we had a nine-acre field of marrow stem kale which grew to a height of three feet, six inches to four feet. Ideal cover for birds and foxes. It would usually take a good pack of hounds to make the fox leave that cover so, what chance Scraggy on his own? People with guns thought I was mad when I asked them to take positions (stands) around the field, as Scraggy would work the kale on his own. Foxes, or a fox, if there, would break cover driven by Scraggy. You could see the look of disbelief on their faces, as they thought they would be wasting their time. During the season, seven foxes were shot by this method. WHAT A DOG! He made the impossible - possible.

※

On another occasion, on a bitter cold day shooting in the marshes at Vellator, just off the coast at Saunton, someone dropped a teal in the dyke (salt water) which Scraggy soon retrieved. Within minutes, his face and coat were covered in ice! This was really frightening. We took him to the car and started the engine, turned on the heater and roared up the engine. After what seemed hours (was really only minutes) Scraggy began to thaw out.

As it was getting late, we decided to call it a day and make for a pub in Braunton, named The Agricultural Inn, where we knew a huge log fire would be burning and where the (still very cold) dog could lie and warm up. His master and friends could partake of some whisky, to warm themselves from the bitter cold.

There is one incident that I think I should tell you about. Scraggy and I were there, but were in no way involved. It happened during the very hard winter and frosts of 1967. We had been shooting at Stag's Head, Filleigh. The ponds were all frozen over, so no Duck but quite a few Woodcock were about, and the odd pheasant.

We had finished rather early, and on the way back to the pub some silly fool decided to shoot at the ice, in the middle of the pond. What an idiot! The shots hit the thin ice in the middle and sent bits of fine ice flying up into the air. The dogs nearby, thinking something had dropped, then took off across the ice to a spot in the middle, and promptly fell through. They were stuck there in icy water, about twenty yards from the bank, unable to get out. Every time they put their front paws on the ice and tried to pull themselves out, their paws slipped and back they went into the very cold, icy water. What were we to do? I raced back to a spot where the foresters had been sawing logs, hoping to find a rope or some flat pieces of off-cut, but no luck. Nothing. Then I had the bright idea to take one of the wooden gates, throw it on to the ice, and hope we would be able to slide and push, with long poles, far enough out to be able to reach the dogs. Two of us set off to fetch the gate. By the time we got back to the pond, some two or three minutes, 'R' had stripped off boots and shooting jacket, had grabbed a small oak branch about three feet long, and was on the edge of the pond beating the ice in a frenzied way. Then, into the freezing water, beating and smashing a path towards the dogs trapped out in the middle. Perhaps it is right to point out that this pond was twelve feet to thirty feet in depth.

'R' was breaking the ice, about half an inch thick, and edged slowly nearer to the dogs. We just looked on, helplessly, watching the drama unfold before us. 'Pray God that he makes it'. I found myself clenching my fists. He is nearly there. Another five feet and he has made it. He turns. The dogs follow. Would they make it back? He had made it about half-way back and we could see the weight of his clothes, and the bitterly cold water was taking effect on him. His strokes became more laboured and slower - still ten yards to go. 'Come on 'R', come on, you're nearly there'. It was going to be touch and go. Two of the guns stood at the water's edge, one arm around a sapling tree and the other outstretched to grab 'R'. Two more strokes, although rather feeble and weak, their hands met. I think we all shouted with joy and relief. We had a struggle to get him up the steep bank. We managed to knot two strong woollen scarves together and get them around his back and under his arms. Two people on the end of the scarves, with two pulling him by his wrists, and we managed to slowly haul him up the bank. The dogs followed close behind. 'R' was nearly too weak and cold to walk. I think we more or less carried him to The Stags Head some fifty yards away. We always had a warm-up and a cup of tea, when we had finished shooting, around a huge log fire.

We got 'R' as far as the fire; held him up and stripped off his icy, sodden clothes. We held him naked in front of the fire. The landlord brought us towels, and we set to work rubbing him down and trying to get his circulation going. The rest of us started stripping off, to provide him with dry, warm clothes. I took off my long-johns; someone gave a vest; someone else, a shirt; another, a roll-neck sweater and someone found a pair of dry socks. What people would have thought had they seen us, half undressed, I do not know. We were not a pretty sight!

I suppose this took about twenty minutes. Colour was returning to his face and he had stopped shivering. We had won. The landlord brought us hot tea and coffee.

We had dried the dogs off and put them in the back of the Landrover, on deep straw. When the boys took the gate back, they looked over at the pond and it had already iced over again - showing how bitterly cold the water was and how brave and lucky 'R' had been.

I felt drained, as I am sure we all did. What had happened in the last half an hour could have been a great disaster. Someone up there was on our side that day. I think we had just seen a miracle. 'R' was going to be all right, and so were the dogs.

As for the chap who fired his gun and caused all the trouble, I'm sure he learnt his lesson, and won't make the same mistake again.

❋

Scraggy, the wild one. Despite his name, he was really a good-tempered dog. He was very soft and soft mouthed, as proved by his retrieving (never a bird torn by him) but, when roused, a really tough character.

I remember, one day, rabbitting on a neighbour's farm. The owner, a friend of mine, warned me that his dog was a devil for fighting, so advised me not to let Scraggy go near him. I knew the 'wild one' could look after himself, so I forgot about the warning. While ferreting a burrow near the farmyard their dog, renowned for his fighting, appeared and, without warning, set upon Scraggy. In a very sort while he realised his great mistake. Scraggy grabbed him in a very painful spot and gave him a couple of bites. Whereupon, in great pain and having been taught a lesson, retreated to the safety of the yard not to be seen again that day! Another day, was when I was not there and he was away with Ray, a friend. While walking down a country road, he was suddenly set upon by a huge mongrel dog being exercised by two ladies. He grabbed the dogs by the hind quarters and refused to let go. The only way Ray could make him let go was by breaking his gun, removing the barrels, putting them in Scraggy's mouth and using them as a lever to open his mouth, and release the other dog. The ladies were in tears but they in no way blamed Scraggy, as they knew it was their dog that had started it.

❊

When waiting for ducks to flight or pigeons to come home to roost, one did not have to look skywards but just watch the dog, who seemed to hear or scent their approach (in the case of the pigeons, it must have been hearing). When he moved his head and looked skywards, you were pretty sure a bird or birds were coming from that direction. When one was shot, off he would go, bringing it back to your feet and then sit again, ready for the next one. We usually finished our day's rough shooting, when away from home, at a pub on the way home. I well remember one day when it had been raining all the afternoon. We reached one of the pubs, which we always called in at when shooting in that area. We had ordered our drinks when the landlord, asked where my dog was - he was the only dog on that particular shoot. I told him that I had rubbed him as dry as possible, and he was snug in a bale of straw in the back of the Landrover. He, the landlord, a very kind and jolly man, insisted that I fetch him and sit him in front of a blazing fire. This he persuaded me to do. Although I was sure he was more comfortable in his deep nest of straw in the Landrover, than he would be in front of the fire, on a hard stone slab floor. He had not been in long when he, Scraggy, got up and went behind the Bar and cocked his leg over one of the beer barrels (wooden in those days). The landlord had left the bar to answer the telephone. Luckily, I had forgotten to take out an old scarf which was in the pocket of my shooting jacket, that was draped over a chair, drying out. I grabbed the scarf, mopped up the mess from the stone floor, and by the time the landlord came back, Scraggy was lying like an angel in front of the fire. 'There,' said the Landlord, 'I told you he would be far better in here'. My friends gave me a wry smile, and we all had another beer.

❊

I think this story would not be complete, unless I mentioned a few of the characters that I shot with at his time. Those who came to know Scraggy so well. They were a mixed bunch of people, with far different outlooks on life and very different careers. But they all had one thing in common, their love of country life and country sports. They enjoyed a drink at the end of a day's shoot. A bottle of port at lunch-time, when stories of past shooting days were told - (perhaps with little bits added here and there)!

TOM O. - who had a distinguished Army career during the last war, where he was mentioned in dispatches for his bravery. He had an old hammer gun, nicknamed 'Betsy' (I don't know why), with Damascus barrels. He was a great shot at high pigeons. He used to call his dog with a silent whistle, which humans were unable to pick up as it had a very high and shrill tone, but the dogs could

Lunchtime at the Stag's Head - the morning's bag.

hear. Thus the name, 'Silent Whistle'. He was great fun to be with and when he had had a few, would often burst forth into song.

Tom and I had a yearly challenge. It was nothing much, really, but to us it was a thing on which we both took a great pride in winning. At any time, from about the middle of the month of May, we could challenge the other to dig up three roots of new potatoes, from his garden, and me from mine. They would be weighed at the same time, and the winner was presented with a bottle of whisky, by the loser. This usually took up a complete Sunday morning. 'R' and 'C' came along to act as umpires, to see fair play and to partake of the bottle of whisky. By the time we left, we usually managed to leave the winner a small drop in the bottom, to celebrate his victory later on. I think, over a period of eight to ten years, we finished about level on victories. When you won, those spuds tasted extra good.

MAJOR, E. - a great character - a Yorkshireman. He was landlord at a Yar Down pub, the Poltimore Arms. He ran this with the aid of his sister, an ex-W.A.F. Officer, with a very deep voice. Still rather military in her manner but, when you really got to know her, a friendly and even motherly sort of person. She was a great cook. We often had meals there, when shooting with the Major at Alswear.

The Stag's Head, scene of many happy hunting days.

Major was 'his own man'. His upright military figure, his typical Major's moustache, his booming voice and his liking of young people. He always tried to keep young. We all respected him for his humour, his tales of bygone days (told week after week), and his excitement as he told those tales after a hearty lunch, and a bottle of port. The spittle used to run down the stem of his pipe, when he was in full flow. His black labrador 'Barker', a very friendly dog, was not a great deal of use in the shooting field. To him he was a great dog. Where the Major was - there would be 'Barker'.

Then there was DOC. - In charge of the shoot at the Stags Head, Filleigh. He, too, was a man with great enthusiasm and push, in everything he did.

He had a lot to do in helping to get our new hospital built. He was a member of Barnstaple Town Council, and had to be driving himself hard to get any satisfaction out of life. On shooting days, with his dog, he pushed himself to the limit. Beating and driving out birds to his friends. Most days he would have scratches on his hands, and often on his face, as he charged through the thickest of scrub. Everything he did, he put his all into.

In the end he paid the price. He had a mammoth heart attack, and although he partially recovered, sadly was never able to shoot again, although his wife used to bring him to the Stag's Head for lunch. He could stand in the car park and watch us shoot birds risen from the mound beyond the pond. Very, very sad for a man who had, in the past, been the driving force of Stag's Head shoot, and a leading light for North Devon in many ways. Three special men, now long gone, who loved and understood the countryside and its ways. I was lucky to have known them and shot with them. With me, they left a deep and lasting impression. There was R. and C., two auctioneers, by trade, and many farming friends too numerous to name. They were terrific days, and great chaps.

I think Frank said it all, when drawing a blank in one of his woods, 'We should have had Scraggy here. Even if there was nothing there he would have found something'.

What a tribute!

When sometime there comes the day,
It's time to put your gun away,
Memories of days long gone
Will never fade, but linger on.

PART THREE

~ POEMS ~
REFLECTIONS OF A LIFE

THE SUNSET

The sun sinks low in the West
A ball of deep, red fire,
On the ridge of the hill it rests
Twix the trees and the old church spire.

The mist creeps up the valley,
Silent and whitish-grey,
The air finds a damp, cold chill,
As it slowly goes by on its way.

Birds chant their gay lullabys,
In notes soft, sweet and low,
From trees hanging dry and parched,
In the sunsets deep, red glow.

The shadows grow long and deep
In the fast fading light,
Not a sound fills the still air
Breezes alone stir the night.

May, 1941

A GARDEN OF DREAMS

I've planted my heart in a garden of
   dreams,
A sweet paradise for two,
'Neath the shade of the trees and
   flowers,
I planted it there for you.

I planted it there in the winter of life,
When the world was so cold and bare,
Waiting and longing for spring-time,
With sunshine and skies so fair.

Then fate came along to my garden of
   dreams,
The skies turned from grey to blue,
The sun shone from out the heavens,
As my heart burst in bloom for you.

Now fate is a beautiful lady,
Soft and sweet as the dew,
Stay in my garden for ever,
Springtime always with you.

1942

THE STORM (Sonnet)

The heavens seem filled with darkness,
Gaunt black clouds roll over-head,
Not a breeze stirs the air,
The whole world seems dead.

The silence is shattered by thunder,
Lightening streaks to its prey,
Rains lash down in fury,
Fed by those clouds of prey.
Then nature springs to life,
The sun comes glinting through,
Trees shake themselves in the breeze,
The grass has a silvery hue.
Little birds begin posing,
Lambs start to frisk and play,
Flowers raise their heads to the sunlight,
The storm has passed away.

1942

MEMORIES

One day, not long ago,
A day of toil and strain,
Fate chanced to pass my way,
As I met you again.

Years ago, when we met,
The world was gay and bright,
We waltzed, just you and I,
And fell in love that night.

The sun will shine again,
The dark clouds roll away,
We'll live in memories,
Until that dawn of day.

Memories still linger on,
Memories will never depart,
Memories I hold dear to me,
The secrets of my heart.

1941

MY DOG

Bob, though a bit of a mongrel,
Was the best in the world to me,
A white, curly coat, two brown eyes,
I often still fancy I see.

Bob was a grand little fellow,
My best pal for nigh thirteen years,
He was always there, my best friend,
In days filled with sorrow and tears.

We'd hunt together, Bob and I,
In summer we'd toil through the heat,
In winter the cold wet thicket,
At even the fire, at my feet.

One day while hunting the grassland,
A rabbit sprang out of a dell,
I swung my gun on the target,
Bang, my gun dropped, Bob stumbled and fell.

I raced to the spot where he lay,
A small, crumpled heap on the grass,
One wag of his small stumpy tail,
Tears fell as I knew twas his last.

I cursed myself with a vengeance,
As gently I stroked his soft hide,
For his love of true sport he lived,
By my hand and my gun, he died.

I laid him to sleep 'neath the beech,
As autumn leaves fell with a sigh,
Soft, sweet smelling moss for his bed,
One last look, Bob, my Bob goodbye.

OCTOBER, 1943

SPRING

The bareness of winter finds new life,
As spring unfolds upon a world of pain,
Slowly nature wakes from out her
    slumber,
'Roused by warm sunshine and light
    showers of rain.

Spring, your magic spell fills our hearts
    with joy,
Ragged hedgerows are decked with buds
    of green,
So small and yet so inhumanly perfect,
A hundred different shapes and hues are
    seen.

Birds fill the soft morning air, with gay
    song,
O what great hopes each note foretells,
At dusk small furry balls of life appear,
As rabbits scamper quickly o'er the dells.

We hear the harsh chant of the
    rookeries,
Or the babbling stream rushing down
    the hill,
The miracle of spring will never fade,
Through endless years its joys our hearts
    will fill.

NOVEMBER, 1943

INSTRUMENTS (Xmas Games)

Instruments of good or evil,
Instruments for peace or strife,
Man leaves his character behind,
As he journeys on through life.

Instruments of joy or sadness,
In this world so tired and torn,
Instruments of war so cruel,
Kill the hopes that once were born.

Instruments of love or hatred,
Through this world go side by side,
Sometimes peaceful, sometimes restless,
Like an ever moving tide.

Through the ages marching forward,
Oh! what joy to man should bring,
But jealousy and oft' malice,
Crush the hopes to which they cling.

JANUARY, 1944

A TREE

Against the western sunset glow,
The gnarled and twisted fir doth stand,
Battered by a thousand great storms,
Its roots set deep down in the land.
Its arms outstretched to highest heaven,
Its head sways gently in the breeze.
Oh! glorious rugged splendour,
That alone we see in trees.

Through winter cold and summer heat,
In storms and calm you've slower grown,
From sapling to a mighty tree,
Where two small love-birds build their
    home,
Oh tower of strength and beauty,
Untouched, unspoilt by lowly man,

Through endless years you've stood there,
A small part of God's great plan.

JANUARY, 1944

WINTER

Winter, season of rest and peace
When nature's life for a time shall cease,
The harvest done, its fruits safely in store,
Winter comes with a rush and a roar.
Giant trees battle grimly with the gale,
As it sweeps unchecked on hill and dale,
The swollen river swirls madly by,
Beneath the sullen, windswept sky.

All birds have lost their lust for song,
For them, bleak winter is cruel and long.
Their food is now so hard to be found,
Pure white snow lies lightly on the ground.

Yet how good sounds, the huntsman's horn,
Echoing through woods on a frosty morn.
Horses hoofs on the frozen land,
The bay of the hounds so close at hand.

✤

At even', beside the blazing fire,
Sweet tobacco smoke and pale blue spire,
Heads nod slowly in the firelight glow,
Tired of body, content of soul.

JANUARY, 1944

WE WHO ARE DEAD

We who are dead, our task is done,
We hate nor weep no more,
We live in peace beyond all hope,
Safe behind heavens door.

Only your sad and weeping hearts,
Can cause us any pain,
Weep not for us ye that are left,
For death has been our gain.
Just live a good and upright life,
In your sad world below,
For we shall meet again up here,
Where tears can never flow.

MAY, 1944

THE CONSCIENCE OF A SINNER

Am I damned to hell for ever,
Have I sinned enough for this?
Are my dreams all shattered, broken,
Had I power to resist?

For just one slight slip in life,
Must I damn and break stout hearts
Of those who love me dearly,
Must I tear their lives apart?

Is there no loving God on high
To Him my earnest prayer,
If not for me, for them forgive
Or else my hell they'll share.

"Forgive me God", is my cry,
Every moment of the day,
My only hope now lies in You,
Give me the power to pray.

MAY, 1944

LOVE

Love most fragile and lovely flower of all,
How oft' does jealousy bring about thy fall?
Yet raise again thy head above all strife,
For without love there is no life.
Let thy sweet scent fill the evening air,
Let thy gay blooms shine everywhere,
Oh! love never more didst the world need thee,
For without love there's no hope for me.

MAY, 1945

JEALOUSY

How oft' does jealousy raise its head
To review bitter memories that were dead?
To stir up hatred and great strife,
Perhaps to ruin many a life.

Jealousy, most hatred foe of us all,
Who gloats as dreams, shattered, fall
But love will defeat thy armed might,
So go, jealousy, you have lost the fight.

MAY, 1945

SO FEW

So few, in those dark days, of bitterness and pain
When France fell at a blow, and when Hitler's power did reign,
Remember 1940? The world was sad and drear,
But the courage of those few, taught us not to fear.

So few, and yet enough to smash those swarms of huns,
Just a tiny handful of Britain's gallant sons
Each day they flew the heavens, each day new victories won
Each day those fiends wavered before your stuttering guns.

So few, yet our whole land bore witness of the fight,
Twisted heaps of metal were Göerings boasted might,
Against gigantic odds, you never were subdued,
You feared not them nor death, your land in peril stood.

So few, and yet so much lay grasped within their hand,
Many a man gave all in that undying stand,
Victors of Britain's skies, your valour victory gained,
Your spirit will forever live, immortal and unstained.

MAY, 1943

YELLOW ENVELOPE

A cold, dull night in December,
The fog lay closed with the ground,
The postman's steps on the street,
Were the only human sound.

A shrill bell breaks the silence,
As he stops at No. 10 door,
Ann rises up from the fireside,
And silently crosses the floor.

She gropes her way down the passage,
The air feels cold and damp,
Her face looks wan and tired,
In the light of the pale blue lamp.
She curses the blackout softly,
As she switches on her small torch,
Her body gives a quick shudder,
The postman stood there 'neath the
  porch.

Bob's been missing for weeks now,
Since the 51st broke through,
Is he prisoner or dead,
O God, which of these two is true?
Ann knows the answer lies hidden,
Beneath that small envelope flap,
No wonder she gives a shudder,
Will joy or despair fill the gap?

For a moment Ann stands quite still,
Then walks slowly back to her chair,
The fire burst into dull flame,
Casting deep shadows everywhere.
Grimly she tears off the flap,
Jerks fate from out his hide,
Her small hands quiver and tremble,
As she reads through the lines inside.

Her hands are steady now,
Her eyes have a vacant stare,
Her lips move unconciously,
As she murmers a little prayer.
Out there in the thirsty desert,
With its seemingly endless sand,
Bob sleeps in immortal slumber,
'Neath a scarred plot of parched land.

She raises her face to the light,
As bright tear-drops glisten there,
Jim starts to cry in his cot,
Craving his mother's care.
He stops as she picks him up,
     Thank God he's too young to know,
The hellishness of bloody war,
Which has crushed his mother's soul.

Twenty-two years have rolled between,
Tho' it seems but yesterday,
Jim's grown to a fine man now,
So much like his brave dad, they say,
The world has healed all its deep
  wounds,
Her sons are so happy and free,
Thanks to the men like Private Bob,
Who died that their sons may be free.

DECEMBER, 1942

MY COUNTRY'S CALL

I answer my Country's call to do my bit you
  see,
Side by side with blokes who fight, out
  there for you and for me,
I'm proud to answer her call, to help to
  defend the free,
For it's better to die in battle than lose your
  liberty.

Europe cries out in anguish beneath the nazi yoke,
Her eyes turn to Britain, her only remaining hope.
We shall not let them down in the air, on land or on sea,
We shall fight 'till we've beat the hun and gained the right to be free.

So until the battle's o'er, until the world is free.
Until Europe once more regains her liberty,
It's an honour to the Empire, to blokes like you and me,
To fight or die for freedom, so on to glorious victory.

JUNE, 1940

THE N.F.S.

Firemen of Great Britain,
Whose hearts are brave and true,
Heroes of the home front, we owe a lot to you,
Your courage and grim endurance, the pride of the free,
Yours is the fighting spirit of our great democracy.

In the midst of blazing hells, while bombs came screaming down,
Half choked by smoke and fumes you fought to save our towns.
From tops of swinging ladders or beside bomb-scarred walls,
You fought choking smoke and flames, hanging on by guts and claws.

All through the firelit night, you toiled and laboured long.
Defying death and fire you kept your hoses on,
The fires spat back in fury, being robbed of their prey,
But you never failed or faltered till those flames had died away.
Behind the old grey church, there's a little earthen mound,
Just a crude bare wooden cross, stuck there in the ground.
His name was Fireman Roberts
Killed by a crumbling wall,
A hero of the home front, now gone, beyond recall.

OCTOBER, 1940

STALINGRAD

Soldiers of Stalingrad, comrades of the free,
With supremist courage, you fought for liberty,
With your backs to the Volgar, hemmed in by the huns,
All your bridges blown to hell, by half a million guns.
Bleeding, torn and tired, no respite day or night,
Half dazed by cold and hunger, battered by Hitler's might,
Your courage never wavered, you grimly faced the foe,
Desperately you clung on, and stemmed their onward flow.

Amidst your shattered ruins, dyed crimson with your blood,

The bloody battle raged, in Autumns icy
   flood,
With unrelenting fury, fought out street by
   street,
Each house held till, to the last, for you no
   word retreat.
In factories, in graveyards, laid waste by cruel
   war,
Mere words can ne'er describe, the sufferings
   you bore.
Never, in all wars, was so great a sacrifice
   made,
The epic of Stalingrad will never, never fade.

Against the star-lit sky, your city stands
   forlorn,
Your noble streets are shattered, tragic,
   shapeless, torn.
Your sons lie sleeping, silent, great was the
   price they paid
Their spirit, through tortured Russia, restless
   proud doth wade.
The huns are reeling back, before your
   comrades blows,
The blood of Stalingrad sons, onward still
   onward flows.
Westward ever westward, sweeping o'er hills
   and plains,
Cleansing their fatherland, of foul inhuman
   stains.

NOVEMBER 1943

DOTH BRITAIN STILL WAGE WAR?

   The pits lie idle, silent,
   Doth Britain still wage war?
   Are her brave sons still dying?
   Is she rotten to the core?

In the air on land or sea,
Men sweat and toil in blood,
The blood of brothers fallen,
Engulfed beneath the flood.

Yet some men prefer to strike,
No blood they're asked to spare,
Only just to back them up,
Our boys fighting out there.

For every moment that's last,
Some men the price must pay,
Some small kid must lose his dad,
All for a bob a day.

When you're on strike again,
Go to the Docks and see,
A Red Cross ship in berth there,
Watch a minute with me.

A man goes by, his sight gone,
The next will walk no more,
Oh! endless and tragic line,
Men maimed by cruel war.

Yet they smile as they go by,
They know not who you are,
Go to your job and stick it,
It's you that they've fought for.

APRIL, 1944

CHRISTMAS DAY 1943

Christmas dawns on a world of pain,
Where war doth rage and ill doth reign,
Yet for this day all strife shall cease,
Thoughts turn to home, to love and
   peace.

Many homes are sad and broken,
Many thoughts are left unspoken,
In the still, chill morning air,
Many heads are bowed in prayer.
Yet on this day new hopes arise,
The sun appears through cloudy skies,
And God's world, tho' bitter and torn,
Finds peace and hope on Christmas morn.

DECEMBER, 1943

EASTER 1944

Waiting for the bugle, the British Tommy stands,
Waiting to cross the sea to rescue other lands,
Memories of Dunkirk still linger in their brain,
Their one thought now revenge, revenge for comrades slain.
With the same determined spirit armed to fight,
They clamly wait the hour to strike with all their might.
When ere that day shall dawn and hell breaks loose out there
May God protect our lads, must be our earnest prayer.

Revenge will be their cry, struggling up beaches bare,
On through withering fire, many men have a one-way fare.
Yet on they'll trudge through living hell, grimly up the road,

'Till freedoms light shall shine again, they'll bear their heavy load,
'Till millions of tortured minds once again are free,
Free to live and think in their world, now slavery.
heir task will be hard and long, no easy road they'll tread
Ere autumn's leaves shall fall sleeping, so lightly dead.

APRIL, 1944

VICTORY

Soon that great day shall dawn, that day of Victory,
Throughout the world freedom's flags unfurl in glorious magesty.
When bonds shall snap and fetters break, the peoples shall be free,
The boys return to the lands they love, the lands of Liberty.
Some will return to cottage, some to mansion grand,
But all to home, to love and peace in their dear native land.

MAY, 1945

PROGRESS?

I sit beneath the pale, blue sky
And dream and let the world pass by,
I think of all those bye-gone years
Of cloud and sunshine, joy and tears.

Of days when I was just a lad,
Of all the fun and games I had,
Many things we used to play,
Just to pass the time away.

Those days when time, did not matter much,
You still got there, no need to rush.
You slowly, gently, went your way,
'Twas all the same at end of day.

The countryside was full of life,
So peaceful, far away from strife.
Many men were working there,
The land was safe with all their care.

The laughter, talking, now all gone
With machinery, the work is done.
The roar and sight of huge machines,
This is now the country scene.

Progress too long, you've had your way,
Then comes the time when we must pay.
No shops or schools can be found there,
Village life's now empty, cold and bare.

The cottages where workers dwelt
Are now all in the tourist belt.
No part of country life are they,
They're mostly let for holiday.

It's now time to end this dream
Of what was once the country scene.
The light is fading in the west.
Best go in, it's time to rest.

APRIL, 1996

ODES

AN ODE TO OLD SHOOTING CHUMS

When I was asked to your shoot dinner
I don't know if it's as saint or sinner?
Perhaps an ode about you all
Is the reason for the call

Our girls are with us here tonight
Don't they make a pretty sight
Your thanks to them is long o'er due
When they do so much for you.

This I will now try to do
To say nice things 'bout all of you
Remember that I know your past
The truth will now come out at last!

Arthur May the Keeper is
It's up to him to make things fizz
He puts the birds over your head
It's not his fault if they're not dead.

There are lots more of the 'Mays'
Who are oft' there on shooting days
On shooting, they're all completely mad
For the birds, this news is sad.

I suppose that I should say
I am entangled with a 'May'
Her love and care cannot be bad
For Fifty year she's kept her lad.

Then there's Frank with his three dogs
Who's always ready for a slog
He works his dogs so well all day
Is greatly missed when he's away.

Then there is that dentist chap
Who never seems to fret or flap
He just gets on and shoots the birds
Is very seldom lost for words.

We also have his better half
Who's always ready for a laugh
She picks up birds that you have shot
Is most important of the lot!

Then there is a chap called Ray
Who enjoys his shooting day
He quietly goes and takes his stand
Content to do the job in hand.

Another chap whose name is Crang
Simply can't resist a bang
Sometimes he makes the feathers fly
Especially if the bird's not high!

Alan, one of the older hands
Who sometimes grumbles at his stand
But at the next he fires a lot
His moans and groans are soon forgot.

A new Gun that I don't know
Is now a member of your show
I think he is a man called Dart
I'm sure that he will fit the part!

Then there is my old pal, Jim
A fine shoot member he has b'n
He does so much in many ways
He deserves to enjoy his shooting days.

Then there is that Johnny Hill
Who simply can-not stand still
One day when on a walk-about
A pellet made him jump and shout!

Then there is your Chair Man
Who welcomes men of every Clan
He wishes them 'Bon Chance, Good day'
But for some, keeps well out the way!

Then Tony that crack clay-bird shot
He doesn't seem to miss a lot
But even he gets an off day
When birds are glad they flew his way!

Then there is another John
Who's not been in the Shoot for long
A very important man is he
For he does the Treasury!

Then you have two Han-cocks
They seem to have a dead slow clock
On shooting days they're often late
But usually arrive on right date.

An ex Copper, a grand chap
He helps the Shoot, does this or that
He sometimes shoots, been known to miss
Sometimes the Beaters does assist.

I think you have another guest
His name is Des, one of the best
We've had a few drinks in the past
His kind of friendships one to last.

And last but not least is our friend Joe
A great sportsman, from head to toe
He only is 80 odd years young
His eye still good, his heart still strong.

There's one or two that I have missed
They simply were not on my list
I know one from days gone by
The other is a Keeper guy.

Then I must remember David and
   Stephanie
We're always welcome there for tea
We're often dirty, wet and cold
Their roaring fire a sight to behold!

There is one thing more that I must say
To thank you for my Shooting Day
A few birds flew into my shot
But somehow I still missed the lot.

You really are a mixed up lot
Yet every one has his own slot
You do your jobs on Shooting days
With your own pet whims and ways.

And when sometime there comes the day
It's time to put your gun away
Memories of days long gone
Will never fade, but linger on.

1995

THAT GAME OF GOLF!

The other day with nowt to do
I wrote an ode 'bout me and you
Our moods and whims, how they change
When we play a certain game.

When looking round, it's plain to see
A bunch of chaps, nice as can be
But place a golf club in their hand
They become a raving luny band.

The ladies, on the other hand
Are a far, far, nicer band
They walk together, chat a lot
Been known to say, "What a good shot".

You place your golf ball on the tee
That's the end of chivalry!
The war is on, no word is spoken
Silence reigns, friendships are broken.

He hit the ball with all his might
And watched in horror at its flight
The shot he hit, a wicked hook
The damned things landed in the brook.

He curses, swears, but not at you
He knows he did not follow through
His partner, with a softer blow
Chips on the green, to half the hole.

When later on he fluffs a shot
He throws his clubs, and swears a lot
What this is supposed to do, I don't know
And now do you.

A golf ball, I'd hate to be
With the golf vocabulary
To cut, bend, fade, hook, get in!
Must get bewildered by the din.

And when at last it's had enough
It hides itself, deep in the rough
There to take a well-earned rest
It's not its fault, it did its best!

At last we reach the 18th green
And pause to think what could have been
The ball that rolled in that deep dip
The putt that stopped right on the lip.

The match all square, both there in two
It's your first putt, it's up to you
The putt rolls in, your joy is rife
Theirs drops too, the end of strife.

You're tired and weary; take a shower
You've been out there for nigh five hour
Out there in that incessant heat
You tried so hard, you feel dead beat.

Refreshed at bar, you laugh and chat
About nothing much, just this and that
The tension gone, you're friends once more
The game of golf - Oh! What a bore!!

1995

AN ODE TO GOLFING WIDOWS

When you tell us, how mad we must be
To leave our home and sanctuary
To play golf, get soaked through
When we did it just for you.

That's the thanks we often get
For staying out and getting wet
To stay out there in pouring rain
To endure the hurt and pain.

We did it to give you a break and rest
To leave you snuggld in the nest
Warm, peaceful and content
While WE face the elements!

We knew the wet and bitter cold
Would make the clubs so hard to hold
The sacrifice we poor men make
All for our dear wive's sake!

So come what may - rain, sleet and gale
And sometimes even snow and hail
You're glad to see the back of us
So off we go without a fuss.

The afternoon, 'tis now all yours
So now forget the household chores
Why not have a shopping spree?
Then present the bill to me!

To help tell me what you have done
My good temper, first, must be won
You tell me to sit in best armchair
Sit on the arm and stroke my hair.

Now the time is surely right
To give him a financial fright
To tell just what you have spent
To tell where all the money went!

You don't quite know, how to start
How to reach his loving heart
No longer can you the secret keep
But it's too late, he's fast asleep!!

1995

AN ODE TO THE BOBBIES OF NORTH DEVON

I've been asked to write about you Coppers
This gives me chance to tell some whoppers
To say what I really think of you
Maybe false or maybe true.

But anyrate I'll have a go
Rather tedious and slow
Just like you when on the Beat
Can't use my head and seem all feet.

The words just won't come my way
I'll have to leave it for today
Perhaps when I have had a sleep
I'll wake up and this ode's complete.

I've had my sleep and feel refreshed
So now I'll really try my best
To try and look deep into your mind
And be surprised what I shall find.

When your note-book you take out
To write down what it's all about
You have to keep the written laws
With all their foolishness and flaws.

When playing golf you're just the same
You write down handicap and name
You really love to use your pad
For some of you 'tis a proper fad.

Your'e really not a bad lot
Sometimes your copy-book do blot
A blind eye would meet the case
So don't take out your book in haste.

In years gone by I was one of you
Yes, a member of your crew
A Special Cop I used to be
Both sides of law I now can see.

If I could take you to a Court
Your handIcaps I then could sort
You know they're false as they can be
Especially when you're playing me.

When we've had a damned hard game
Somehow we've kept you in the frame
Sometimes you win and sometimes us
A pint of beer becomes a must.

Just a word about our Skipper
Who certainly is no quitter
He plays golf nigh every day
If not at Saunton, then away.

Snooker's a game that he tries too
He simply has not got a clue
He walks round table, mutters a lot
He's just missed an easy pot.

We have a go at potting balls
A game of snooker is the cause
The laughter, banter that's heard - then
Is only heard between good friends.

We all look forward to these days
Such great fun in many ways
A time to let down your hair
Especially if you're not in Chair.

I think it's time to end this rhyme
Before the Landlord calls out, 'Time'
Mine's a tonic with some Gin
You've just got time to get it in.

A great day ends, it's time to go
Your speech is slightly slurred and slow
A good long sleep will put things right
So off we go, into the night.

APRIL, 1996

CHRISTMAS

What does Christmas really mean
Is it just a snowy scene?
Is it time of rest and peace?
When for some all work shall cease.
Or does it mean much more than this
Something that we cannot miss
A time of family festivities
Gathered round the Christmas tree
What a joy it is to be
A united family.

One more thing I'll quickly do
Before I bid you all adieu
May Christmas be your best one yet
A time you never will forget
A new year blessed with joy and peace
May your laughter never cease
May the sun shine down on you
A cloudless sky the whole year through
Good night and God bless.

1995

SPRING EVENING

The day has been a sweltering one, perhaps the hottest ever for May, or the hottest I can remember for this very lovely month.

It is now around eight o'clock, the cool evening when it feels so good to be alive after the sweat of toil during the day.

As the sun sinks lower in the west, I find
...myself walking on the spongy turf of

Codden Hill which, although only about six hundred feet above sea level, stands proud above its neighbouring hillocks.

As I pause in my ascent up its side, how glorious the country seems to be.
"Oh! to be in England, now that spring is here". How true those words are tonight, even though this England is war-torn and spring is somewhat marred by that fact.

Although I've stood here many times before and gazed at 'Exmoor' in the north, 'South Molton' in the East, 'Dartmoor' to the south and in the west, 'Lundy Island', standing dark and bold on a sea of silver. The west, where the sun sinks slowly behind giant trees, whose gigantic shadows stretch half way across the patchwork of fields where small balls of fur frisk and play in the warm evening air.

Tonight, in the peaceful evening, those sights have a new beauty. Tonight, I'm in love.

What two ideals go together better than spring and love?
For spring is the season of love, when birds mate and fill the evening air with gay song as the lark, overhead, is doing at this moment.

As the birds sing and the woods' hedgerows burst forth into new life, our hearts desire to burst forth with the fragrant, fragile and yet so lovely blossoms of love. My gaze wanders to a straggling village, snuggled in the peaceful valley below.

Tonight it seems so different.
My eyes pick out a thatched cottage with roses growing up its walls, so very white in the evening light. Its tiny garden full of sweet scented flowers. A couple of fair-haired kids play on the grass, while their mum and dad gaze with pride at their tiny garden and the kids rolling at their feet, gurgling with laughter.

How good life is to them, this life which was once a long, sought dream is now reality. Maybe they are not rich, but it's spring in their lives and that's worth more than all the gold.
Spring, what else matters?

As I turn around, I look over my home which lies nestled in the south side of the hill. A different sort of beauty greets my eye. The river Taw, a streak of silver twisting and turning in the valley below as if uncertain which is the right course to the Atlantic, glistening in the distance. For its background stands Tawstock Woods, so very fresh in their many shades of pale and deep greens. A small break between the trees and there, 'neath the great oaks, stands the very beautiful Church of Tawstock. What a setting for any church, twix trees so warm, so secluded and peaceful.

Somewhere behind those woods stands Tawstock Village, just one little street - all thatch, so quaint and old and truly a picturesque old Devon village.
It's growing dark now and as I tread the downward path,

I find myself humming a little tune. Light
   and sweet as the gurgling brook. I have
   now reached the field which leads to my
   home. I stop, light my pipe and gaze away
   to the west, as I puff sweet scented smoke in
   the air. My eyes are fixed on the twisted
   fir, just visable on the skyline, against the
   red glow which had once been the sun.

Maybe not a truly handsome tree yet,
   to me,the most enchanting tree in all the
   world.
   Why?

'Neath that tree I found the real Spring.

MAY, 1944

❋

THE FLOWER THAT NEVER BLOOMED

They planted their seeds with such high hopes. They kept them safe and warm to germinate. They nursed them with tender care and love. After a long time the first small tender shoots appeared.

❋

So fragile, so minute and small, they needed your care and protection from the harsh world outside, with all its hopes and disappointments, its joys and sorrows.

❋

Very slowly, they started to grow and take the shape of things to come. Perhaps robust and very strong, or maybe tender, soft and kind. Getting ready to play their part, very small in some role yet unknown.

❋

Excitement grows, between the leaves a small bud appears. What colour will it be? What shape will it take? Perhaps it will have a lovely perfume. Slowly the bud begins to open, the colour is now plain to see but its shape or what it sometime will become, still unclear. You are left to guess its final shape and what kind of flower will finally come into being.

❋

You planted, raised it up with tender care. Watched it grow. You will soon be able to let go and sit back, keeping a watchful eye and admire with deep fulfillment and love, the flower you have helped bring into being.

❋

You leave it in the garden. You will see it again in the evening when you have finished your daily work. Life feels good, the sun is shining. Soon your garden will burst into bloom.

❋

Suddenly your dreams are shattered. Your garden has been broken into. With one foul stroke, one moment of madness, your bud has been cut down and many more nearby, and left there lying helpless, dead, where they had been growing with such hopes and promise.

❋

Where a few hours ago it was a beautiful sight, the buds swaying gently in the breeze, it is now a bare and barren piece of earth, desolate and cold. Your dreams and hopes all gone. You ask yourself, 'Why'? but can find no answer.

❋

You are left with just memories of what might have been. These are things no-one can take away - the belong to you, forever.

❋

They were:-
Your buds that never opened,
Your flowers that never bloomed.

MARCH, 1996 (Dunblane Disaster)